PENGUIN BOOKS

THE BOOK OF LASTS

STRAVROS COSMOPULOS was born in Dorchester, Massachusetts, and has been a nationally and internationally recognized creative director of advertising for more than three decades.

Mr. Cosmopulos has founded five advertising agencies, the first when he was just twenty-five, three of which still bear his name: Hill, Holliday, Connors, Cosmopulos, Inc., of Boston; Cosmopulos, Crowley & Daly, CKG, Inc., of Boston; and Palmer, Cosmopulos, Palmer, Inc., of Elmira Heights, New York.

Mr. Cosmopulos has produced award-winning advertising in both print and television. His awards include Andys, Addys, Clios, and a bronze lion from the Cannes Advertising Film Festival. He was elected to the New England Advertising Hall of Fame, and has been the subject of a profile by the *Wall Street Journal*. He has lectured at more than fifty colleges and universities, as well as at countless marketing, management, advertising, art directors', and creative organizations and clubs nationally and internationally. He has taught graduate-level creative advertising courses at Syracuse University and Marywood College in Pennsylvania, and is the author of numerous articles on advertising creativity and design.

Mr. Cosmopulos is also an artist in a variety of media, including watercolor, acrylic, sewing, sculpture, and furniture making. He presently serves as an advertising, design and marketing consultant to advertising agencies, publishers, and corporations in the United States as well as overseas. He is the founder, chairman, and president for life of the Friends of the Forest, a worldwide organization established to protect the environment against "people educated beyond their intellect."

The Book of Lasts

An Astonishing Collection of Last Acts, Last Laughs, Last Gasps, Famous Last Words, Memorable Finishes, and Other Noteworthy Endings

Stavros Cosmopulos

PENGUIN BOOKS

PENGUIN BOOKS
Published by the Penguin Group
Penguin Books USA Inc., 375 Hudson Street, New York, New York 10014, U.S.A.
Penguin Books Ltd, 27 Wrights Lane, London W8 5TZ, England
Penguin Books Australia Ltd, Ringwood, Victoria, Australia
Penguin Books Canada Ltd, 10 Alcorn Avenue, Toronto, Ontario, Canada M4V 3B2
Penguin Books (N.Z.) Ltd, 182–190 Wairau Road, Auckland 10, New Zealand

Penguin Books Ltd, Registered Offices: Harmondsworth, Middlesex, England

First published in Penguin Books 1995

1 3 5 7 9 10 8 6 4 2

LIBRARY OF CONGRESS CATALOGING IN PUBLICATION DATA

The book of lasts: an astonishing collection of last acts,
last laughs, last gasps, famous last words, memorable finishes, and other
noteworthy endings / Stavros Cosmopulos.
p. cm.
ISBN 0 14 02.3807 7 (pbk.)
1. Curiosities and wonders. 2. World records—Miscellanea.
I. Cosmopulos, Stavros.
AG243.B587 1995
031.02—dc20   95–4774

Printed in the United States of America
Set in Bookman
Designed by Barbara M. Bachman

DEDICATED TO

My mother and father
Thea and Nicholas Cosmopulos
my Uncle Arthur Keykera
my wife, Reneé
my daughter, Thea Cosmopulos
my son, Nick, and his wife, Susan
my grandchildren,
William Andrew Cosmopulos
Ryan Whittaker Cosmopulos

Preface

The world is fascinated by the first of everything, almost to the exclusion of everything else.

What about lasts? They are too often overlooked, and, to me, far more interesting.

Who was the last signer of the United States Constitution?

What was the last song the Beatles recorded?

What was Marilyn Monroe's last movie?

When was the last day of the Civil War?

This book is a compilation of "lasts" from around the world, designed to answer such questions about the last, the final, and the never-again of just about anything.

Many lasts are to be admired, some are to be envied and held up as goals to be achieved, others to be recognized with nostalgia for their passing, but most are simply to be noted and recorded.

As I did research for this book I felt certain that somewhere there was such a record—a secret repository of lasts. I couldn't believe others had not shared my curiosity. Every time I went into a bookstore I held my breath, afraid I'd see a book of lasts sitting smugly on a shelf.

Fortunately for me there hasn't been one yet. My quest has been long and fascinating, tenaciously tracking down elusive lasts or coming upon others by sheer good fortune. This first edition catalogs lasts.

Hopefully it won't be the last.

If you have any lasts you would like to contribute for future editions, please send them to me, Stravros Cosmopulos, at 8 Bridge Street, Norwell, MA 02061.

Acknowledgments

An extra special thanks to my wife Reneé for her patience with my chaos and clutter around the house.

I had the idea for a book of lasts about ten years ago. Recently, while visiting my friend Skip Morrow in Vermont, I told him of my idea for the book, and he encouraged me enough to do a manuscript. Thank you, Skip.

Special thanks go to Janet Bassemir, Mike Pogodzinski, Geroge Karalias, Anne Davey Orr, Judy Lynch, Peter Diem, and Ernie Anastos.

I also want to thank Thea Yvonne Cosmopulos, Susan Thomas Cosmopulos, Nicholas Stavros Cosmopulos, William Andrew Cosmopulos, Ryan Whittaker Cosmopulos, Mark Alexander, Jim Baker, Paul Balmer, Lynn Bannon, Holly Bandoni, Holly Barlow, Deborah Benson, Steve Block, Fred Brenner, Mat Brown, John Bucci, William Bulger, Dan Carney, Tim Cahill, Paul Collins, Jack Connors, Tom Conroy, Norman Crawley, Jeannie Curhan, Kip LaVigne, Gerry LaVigne, Wayne Dickinson, Harry Daly, Tom Demeter, Jack Derby, Lisa Dionne, Ralph DiVito, Dave Dwyer, Jim Fitts, Bernie Flannagan, Bob Fotheringham, Virginia Garbers, Shirley Gelber, Tom Glass, Jerry Golden, Mort Goldstrum, Roberta Greany, Walter Green, Joanne Haimes, Patsy Held, Christie Higgins, Jay Hill, John F. Hodgman, Sister Cor Immaculatum, Anne Ireland, Sally Jackson, Mary Jacques, Roger Jacques, Christine Jacques, Adrian Jacques, Julie Jacques, Pat Jayson, Norman Jenkinson, Deborah Krampf, Rich Kerstein, Bob Kohlbrenner, Jim Kuhn, Stuart Leeds, Donna LeSchander, Michael Lissauer, Judy Gidge Lynch, Steve Lynch, Shirley Martin, Byron Menides, John Menides, Mark Midland, Arthur Milano, Deborah Miller, Thomas Morse, Barbara Mulville, Bill Murphy, Fran O'Halloran, Matt O'Halloran, Jack O'Halloran, Mary Ann Orr, Rena Ouellette, Craig Palmer, Jay Palmer, John Papas, Michael Peirce, Nick Petkas, Nora Perry, Ken Ricklefs, Patricia Ricklefs, Jerry Roche, Bill Roche, Justin Rohrlich, Rita Roosevelt, Pat Ross, Sis Saari, Rachael Selikoff, Laura Soffey, Sara Stashower, John Trew, Vassilios Vamvas, Deborah Van Rooyen, Rosemary Violante, Betsy Wachtel, Dean Wallace, Jon Wardrip, John Webb, Paul Wheeler, Tara Whitehead, Loredona Wilkerson, Alan Woolwine, Xen Zapis.

My gratitude also to the Boston Public Library Research Division and the Norwell Public Library.

Contents

The Book of Lasts

Hollywood Swan Songs
and Final Acts

HUMPHREY BOGART'S LAST GIFT

Bogart's wife, Lauren Bacall, placed a small gold whistle in his coffin. It recalled her line to him in *To Have and Have Not* in 1945: "If you want anything, just whistle. . . ."

THE LAST MARX BROTHER

Minnie Marx, a long-time trouper, had five sons. Three became classic American vaudeville and film comedians: Chico (b. Leonard, 1887–1961), Harpo (b. Adolph, 1868–1964), and Groucho (b. Julius, 1890–1977). Gummo (b. Milton, 1892–1977) and Zeppo (b. Herbert, 1901–1979) joined the Marx Brothers act at different times but made no significant comic contribution. Zeppo was the last surviving Marx brother.

THE LAST MARX BROTHERS ACT

Groucho, Harpo, and Chico last appeared on screen together in 1959 in a *GE Theatre* episode called "The Incredible Jewel Robbery." It was a totally wordless Harpo and Chico story for the first twenty-five minutes. Groucho made a surprise entrance at the end and said, "We aren't talking till we see our lawyer." Harpo gave Groucho his leg, Groucho gave Chico his leg, and the *You Bet Your Life* duck came out of the sky with a "The End" sign. And it was all over.

JAMES DEAN'S LAST RIDE

Driving his Porsche 550 Spyder on California State Highway 46, just before sunset on September 30, 1955, James Dean collided with a 1950 Ford Tudor driven by Donald Turnupseed. Dean's chest was impaled on the steering column and his neck was broken. According to one doctor, Dean died at 5:45 P.M. Dean's passenger, Rolf Weutherich, was thrown from the car and suffered broken arms and legs, but lived.

MICKEY ROONEY'S LAST WIFE

No. 1: Ava Gardner; No. 2: Betty Jane Rase; No. 3: Martha Vickers; No. 4: Elaine Mahnken; No. 5: Barbara Thomason; No. 6: Marcie Lane; No. 7: Carolyn Hockett, and for the last twenty years wife No. 8: Jan Chamberlain. Rooney says, "My last wife. Honest."

JIMMY DURANTE'S LAST WORDS

Jimmy Durante, the beloved American comedian, traditionally ended his television show with "Goodnight, Mrs. Calabash, wherever you are." The identity of "Mrs. Calabash" was a secret until, near the end of his career, Durante revealed that the mystery lady was his wife, Jeanne Olsen, who had died in 1943. She was nicknamed after the owner of a rooming house in Chicago.

CAROL BURNETT'S LAST GESTURE

Carol Burnett's famous gesture was the last thing she would do on each of her television shows: she would pull her right earlobe as a secret greeting to her grandmother, who had raised her.

LAST MOVIE MADE ON THE MGM LOT

They Only Kill Their Masters in 1972.

THE LAST NAME OF BROTHERS ALBERT, HARRY, JACK, AND SAMUEL

Warner. They founded Warner Brothers Motion Picture Studio in 1923.

MARILYN MONROE'S LAST HUSBAND

Marilyn was married three times. Arthur Miller was her last husband, from 1956 until they divorced in 1961.

THE LAST YEAR "HOLLYWOOD" WASN'T THERE

The last time the hill in Los Angeles, California, that houses the giant world-famous letters spelling "Hollywood" was advertisement-free was in 1922. The following year a real estate developer erected the letters "Hollywoodland" to advertise the area. The letters "L-A-N-D" fell off years later and were never replaced.

THE LAST SILENT MOVIE

The Four Feathers was the last silent movie ever made. Paramount had started it before the talkie revolution and finished it in August of 1929. The African location made it too expensive to be reshot into a talkie. The movie starred William Powell, Clive Brook, and Fay Wray. British producer Alexander Korda made a technicolor version in 1939 that became a film classic.

MARILYN MONROE'S LAST MOVIE

The last movie in which she appeared was *The Misfits*, costarring Clark Gable. The 1961 film was written by her husband, Arthur Miller, and directed by John Huston.

THE LAST CHARLIE CHAN MOVIE

In 1949 *Sky Dragon*, the last of the forty-three Charlie Chan movies, was made. From 1931 to 1941 at 20th Century-Fox, and from 1944 to 1949 at Monogram Studios, Warner Oland, Sidney Toler, and, finally, Roland Winters played the Chinese detective with countless wise sayings.

SHIRLEY TEMPLE'S LAST FILM

The leading child actress of the thirties, who made her first film, *The Red-Haired Alibi*, in 1932, made her last movie as a child actress in 1940. But she returned to the screen in 1947 to star in her last film, *Fort Apache*, released in 1948.

SEAN CONNERY'S LAST APPEARANCE AS 007

After a twelve-year hiatus, Sean Connery returned in 1983 to star in his last James Bond movie, *Never Say Never Again*.

JACK HAWKINS' LAST SPEAKING PART

His last film speaking in his own voice was *The Poppy Is Also a Flower* in 1968. After that he had his larynx removed because of throat cancer and learned to speak again through his esophagus, ten words at a time. He continued to act in films until his death in 1973. A mimic was employed to dub a voice indistinguishable from Hawkins' own.

BRUCE LEE'S LAST FILM

The martial-arts legend died of brain hemorrhage during the filming of *Game of Death* in 1973.

BRANDON LEE'S LAST MOVIE

Bruce Lee's son, Brandon, was accidentally shot and killed during the filming of *The Crow*, released in 1994.

GRETA GARBO'S LAST MOVIE

Garbo was the supreme goddess of the movies, a Hollywood legend. In 1941 she made her last movie, *Two-Faced Woman*, a mild farce with a bit of sexual intrigue. She was only thirty-six when she retired.

THE LAST JANE DARWELL MOVIE

Jane Darwell, who won an Academy Award for her performance as Ma Joad in *The Grapes of Wrath*, made her last motion picture appearance in *Mary Poppins* in 1964. Although she only had one line, she charmed the audience by feeding pigeons, sitting on the steps of St. Paul's Cathedral in London.

THE LAST BASIL RATHBONE SHERLOCK FILM

Basil Rathbone last played Sherlock Holmes in *Dressed to Kill* in 1946. Thereafter, Holmes was played by Christopher Lee, Roger Moore, Peter Cushing, Nicholas Rowe, Michael Pennington, and Anthony Higgins.

THE LAST HEPBURN AND TRACY FILM

The last film Katharine Hepburn and Spencer Tracy appeared in together was *Guess Who's Coming to Dinner* in 1967.

ALFRED HITCHCOCK'S LAST HONOR

Alfred Hitchcock, the undisputed master of cinematic suspense, died of a heart attack on April 29, 1980. His last honor was knighthood, bestowed on him by the Queen of England just a few months before his death. Hitchcock's last movie was *Family Plot*, in 1976.

LAST ABBOTT AND COSTELLO "MEET" MOVIE

The comedy team, who split up in 1957, made their last "Meet" movie under the title of *Abbott and Costello Meet the Mummy*.

ROBINSON'S LAST LINE IN *LITTLE CAESAR*

Edward G. Robinson's last line in the 1930 movie *Little Caesar* was "Is this the end of Rico?"

THE LAST MR. MOTO MOVIE
The last Mr. Moto movie was *The Return of Mr. Moto*, made in 1965, starring Henry Silva. The last Mr. Moto movie made starring Peter Lorre as the Japanese detective was *Mr. Moto Takes a Vacation* in 1939.

CITIZEN KANE'S LAST WORD
Citizen Kane's last word on his deathbed in the 1941 classic movie *Citizen Kane* starring Orson Welles is "Rosebud," the name of a sled that Kane had as a child. The film's last line is spoken by Kane's butler. "Throw that junk in," says the butler (played by Paul Stewart) as "Rosebud" is thrown into the fire.

THE LAST LINE IN *THE WIZARD OF OZ*
The last line spoken in MGM's 1939 movie *The Wizard of Oz* is by Judy Garland, who starred as Dorothy: "Oh, but anyway, Toto, we're home! Home! And this is my room . . . and you're here! And I'm not going to leave home ever again, because I love you all! And . . . Oh, Auntie Em, there's no place like home!"

THE LAST WORDS IN *THE ODD COUPLE*
In the 1968 Paramount Studios movie *The Odd Couple*, starring Jack Lemmon and Walter Matthau, the last words were said by Oscar, played by Matthau: "Hey, and boys, boys, boys! Let's watch the cigarette butts, shall we? This is my house, not a pigsty!"

THE LAST TITLE CARD IN *CITY LIGHTS*
In the final dialogue of the 1931 Charlie Chaplin silent movie, *City Lights*, Chaplin as the Tramp asks the blind girl, played

by Virginia Cherrill, "You? You can see me?" She replies, "Yes, I can see now."

THE LAST SCENE IN *RAIDERS OF THE LOST ARK*

In the 1981 Steven Spielberg and George Lucas adventure film *Raiders of the Lost Ark*, starring Harrison Ford, the last scene on screen shows the cover to the wooden crate containing the Ark of the Covenant being nailed down. Stenciled on the top is a message that reads: "TOP SECRET, ARMY INTELLIGENCE #9906753. DO NOT OPEN." The film ends with the crate being carted off into a warehouse filled with identical crates.

THE LAST FILM JAMES DEAN WAS SCHEDULED TO MAKE

The last role James Dean was scheduled to play before he died in 1955 was with Rocky Graziano in *Somebody Up There Likes Me*. The role subsequently went to Paul Newman.

THE LAST OF THE WOODEN OSCARS

The last time the Oscar, the Academy Award statuette presented to the winners at the motion picture industry ceremonies, was made of wood instead of metal was during World War II. It was gilded.

THE LAST MOVIE IN WHICH JOHN WAYNE DIES

John Wayne made more than 200 movies in his acting career but he died in only eight. The last one in which he dies was also his last film—*The Shootist*, released in 1976.

THE LAST TIME GROUCHO MARX SAW MARGARET DUMONT

Margaret Dumont, remembered as the archetypal dowager who starred with the Marx brothers in seven of their films, was last seen with Groucho Marx in 1965 just outside a stage door after doing her last show, *The Hollywood Palace*. Margaret was waiting with a bouquet of roses that Groucho suspected she had bought for herself. She died a few weeks later, penniless.

THE LAST DR. KILDARE FILM

Dark Delusion was the last film in the Dr. Kildare series, one of MGM's and Hollywood's most entertaining and successful series (1938–1947).

THE LAST VOICE OF FRANCIS THE TALKING MULE

The first six of the seven *Francis the Talking Mule* movies starred Donald O'Connor, and featured Chill Wills's voice as that of Francis. In the seventh and last movie, Mickey Rooney took Donald O'Connor's place (O'Connor had quit, perhaps because Francis was getting most of the fan mail), and Paul Frees provided the voice of Francis.

THE LAST OF THE THREE STOOGES

The last of the Three Stooges, actually a replacement stooge, died July 3, 1993. Curly-Joe DeRita survived being kicked in the shins, poked in the eye, slapped on the head, and given knuckle sandwiches. Curly-Joe joined the Stooges in the late 1950s, replacing the original Curly, the most popular Stooge (Jerome Howard), who died in 1952. Shemp (Howard) died in 1955, and Larry (Fine) and Moe (Howard) died in 1975.

THE LAST OF JOHN BELUSHI

John Belushi died of a drug overdose at the Chateau Marmont, Friday night, March 5, 1982. The Chateau Marmont is on Sunset Boulevard. Belushi often rented No. 3, a two-bedroom bungalow there.

Television Lasts

THE LAST *HOWDY DOODY SHOW*

The last *Howdy Doody* TV show aired on NBC, September 30, 1960. It premiered late in 1947 and exited thirteen years later after 2,343 performances.

THE LAST BROADCAST OF TELEVISION'S FIRST NETWORK

On August 4, 1958, Dumont, television's first network, came to an end with its last telecast of *Monday Night Fights*. Only five stations carried the Dumont network program feed.

THE LAST *M*A*S*H*

The final episode of *M*A*S*H* was broadcast February 28, 1983, and was titled "Goodbye, Farewell and Amen."

THE LAST ED SULLIVAN SHOW

Ed Sullivan hosted the last *Ed Sullivan Show* on June 6, 1971. The first show had been telecast on June 20, 1948.

Famous Last Words About Television by the Father of Radio

Famous last words by Lee DeForest, father of radio, in 1926: "While theoretically and technically television may be feasible, commercially and financially I consider it an impossibility, a development of which we need waste little time dreaming."

Clarabell's Last Words

Since Clarabell never spoke on the *Howdy Doody* TV show, her last words were also her first. On the final show, September 30, 1960, she said, "Good-bye, boys and girls."

The Last Episode of *Dallas*

May 3, 1991, saw the last new episode telecast. ABC's *Dallas*, which started on April 2, 1978, focused on the struggle for money, power, and love in Texas. It was immensely popular, not only in the United States, but overseas as well, where entire English pubs would empty out as patrons hurried home to watch J. R. Ewing (Larry Hagman) on the telly.

The Last Time I Dreamed of Jeannie

On September 18, 1965, Barbara Eden made her debut as the remarkably well-preserved 2,000-year-old genie with a talent for getting her master (played by Larry Hagman) in hot water. The show was last telecast on September 1, 1970.

The Last of *Gilligan's Island*

Last telecast September 9, 1967. This simple-minded farce (starring Bob Denver, Alan Hale, and Jim Backus) about seven people and their shipwrecked boat, the *Minnow*, premiered on September 16, 1964. According to the theme song, the cruise was scheduled to last only three hours. It was a never-ending source of amusement for viewers that the survivors had packed enough outfits for three years and any number of occasions.

THE LAST "HI HO, SILVER"

The Lone Ranger was last telecast September 12, 1957. The Lone Ranger (Clayton Moore) and his faithful sidekick Tonto (Jay Silverheels) first galloped across the TV screens on September 15, 1949.

THE LAST OF *THE MAN FROM U.N.C.L.E.*

Television's answer to James Bond movies was last telecast January 15, 1968. This show, starring Robert Vaughn and David McCallum, first telecast September 22, 1964, developed a devoted audience and spawned a huge amount of U.N.C.L.E. memorabilia.

THE LAST *STAR TREK*

Last telecast of the original *Star Trek* show was September 2, 1969. Set in the twenty-third century and first beamed out to the public on September 8, 1966, this series chronicled the voyages of the starship *Enterprise*, its crew headed by William Shatner and Leonard Nimoy. The show had one of the most devoted audiences ever, and has spawned three sequel series.

THE LAST *YOU BET YOUR LIFE*

You Bet Your Life, an audience participation show, was last broadcast September 21, 1961. The star and emcee of the quiz show was Groucho Marx.

THE LAST *WHAT'S MY LINE?*

With moderator John Daly at the helm, *What's My Line?* was the longest-running game show in the history of prime-time network television. It started on February 16, 1950, and ran for eighteen seasons, until the last telecast on September 3, 1967.

THE LAST *LATE NIGHT WITH DAVID LETTERMAN*

David Letterman's last show on NBC's *Late Night* was on Friday, June 25, 1993. He moved over to CBS in August 1993 to host *The Late Show with David Letterman*.

THE FUGITIVE LAST EPISODE

The last episode of *The Fugitive*, starring David Janssen, was broadcast on August 29, 1967. Nearly 26 million households tuned in to the last installment, in which the identity of Janssen's nemesis, the one-armed man, was revealed. It was the highest-rated program for a TV series ever—until 83 million people tuned in *Dallas* to find out who shot J.R.

THE LAST ANGEL

The last Angel to join the popular TV show *Charlie's Angels* was Julie Rogers, who signed on for its final season in 1980.

THE LAST *I LOVE LUCY* SHOW

After six seasons the last *I Love Lucy* show starring Lucille Ball and Desi Arnaz aired on September 24, 1961.

THE LAST *LIFE OF RILEY*

The original Chester A. Riley had been created on radio in 1943 by William Bendix. However, when the time came to do the TV series, Bendix was making movies and the opportunity went to young Jackie Gleason instead. It was Gleason's first TV series. He did not catch on, and the program was canceled after only one season. Three years later, the series returned with William Bendix and ran for five years. The last show was aired on August 22, 1958.

THE LAST OF *THE HONEYMOONERS*

The first of the thirty-nine episodes of *The Honeymooners*, starring Jackie Gleason, was broadcast on October 1, 1955. The last show was broadcast on May 9, 1971. The so-called lost episodes, aired much later, were actually compilations of Gleason's TV skits from his show before *The Honeymooners*, edited together to look like episodes of *The Honeymooners*.

THE LAST OF *THE BRADY BUNCH*

The last episode of the popular television family comedy series was titled "The Hair-Brained Scheme" and was broadcast on March 8, 1974. The reruns will probably go on forever.

THE LAST OF *THE WALTONS*

The Waltons, a one-hour down-to-earth family television drama, first aired in September 1972. The series chronicled the Depression-era struggles of a close-knit family of seven children in the Blue Ridge Mountains of Virginia. After nine seasons and eleven Emmys, the last episode was broadcast by CBS on August 20, 1981.

THE LAST *BONANZA*

Bonanza, set in the vicinity of Virginia City, Nevada, during the Civil War years, was the story of the Cartwrights, a boisterous family of ranchers. Widower Ben Cartwright, played by Lorne Greene, was the patriarch of the all-male clan and owner of the thousand-square-mile Ponderosa ranch. The show, which also starred Michael Landon, Dan Blocker, and Pernell Roberts, was last telecast on January 16, 1973, after fifteen years.

LAST IN KLINGONESE

In the language of *Star Trek*'s Klingons, an aggressive race often at odds with the more peaceable Federation, the word "last" is "Oav."

CARMEN MIRANDA'S LAST DANCE

Carmen Miranda, the Brazilian actress and singer, whose trademark was a fruit-covered turban, performed her last song and dance on the Jimmy Durante television show in 1955.

THE LAST TELECAST OF *THE OUTER LIMITS*

The Outer Limits opened each episode with a TV screen showing static and wavy lines. A voice would say: "There is nothing wrong with your TV set. We are controlling transmission. We can control the vertical. We can control the horizontal. For the next hour we will control all that you see and hear and think. You are watching a drama that reaches from the inner mind to the Outer Limits." The final telecast was on Janaury 16, 1965, and people heard the memorable last words of the show. "We now return control of your television set to you."

THE LAST TV "GOOD NIGHT, GRACIE"

Comedienne Gracie Allen, when husband George Burns asked her to "Say good night, Gracie," always replied, with her inimitable logic, "Good night, Gracie." She said it for the last time on their television show in 1964, the year she died.

Famous Last Words

JOSEPH P. KENNEDY'S FAMOUS LAST WORDS
The father of President John, Senator Robert, and Senator Ted Kennedy was once quoted as saying: "I have no political ambition for myself or my children."

P. T. BARNUM'S LAST WORDS
"How were the receipts today at Madison Square Garden?" (April 7, 1891.)

HUMPHREY BOGART'S LAST WORDS
To Lauren Bacall as she left the room for a moment, January 14, 1957: "Good-bye, kid. Hurry back."

WILLIAM PALMER'S VERY LAST WORDS
"Are you sure it's safe?" murderer William Palmer asked when he stepped on the trap door of the gallows just before he was hanged.

FERDINAND FOCH'S FAMOUS LAST WORDS

The French marshal was supreme commander of Allied forces during World War I. A few years before the war he said: "Airplanes are interesting toys, but have no military value."

LAST WORDS FROM DEATH ROW

Fifty-four-year-old G. W. Green was executed in the State of Texas in 1991. His last words to his executioner were very simple: "Lock and load. Let's do it."

IRVING THALBERG'S FAMOUS LAST WORDS ABOUT *GONE WITH THE WIND*

Irving Thalberg said to Louis B. Mayer, head of MGM, when he was considering a bid for the screen rights to *Gone with the Wind*: "Forget it, Louis. No Civil War picture ever made a nickel."

THE LAST WORDS OF WINSTON CHURCHILL

The last words Winston Churchill said after a very full lifetime of words were "I'm bored with it all." He then slipped into a coma and died nine days later on January 24, 1965.

FAMOUS LAST WORDS

"I will never marry again," said heiress Barbara Hutton after divorcing the second of her seven husbands.

THE LAST WORDS OF KARL MARX

As Karl Marx lay dying, his housekeeper urged him to tell her his last words so she could write them down for posterity.

Marx, in a cantankerous mood, shooed his housekeeper away with these last words: "Go on, get out—last words are for fools who haven't said enough."

THE LAST WORD ON THE HORSELESS CARRIAGE

Famous last words printed in the *Literary Digest*, 1889: "The horseless carriage is at present a luxury for the wealthy; and although its price will probably fall in the future, it will never, of course, come into as common use as the bicycle."

OLIVER CROMWELL'S LAST WORDS

The last words of Oliver Cromwell, the English statesman, who died in 1658, were: "My desire is to make what haste I may to be gone."

THOMAS EDISON'S LAST OBSERVATION

The last observation of one of the world's greatest inventors, Thomas Edison, as he passed out of existence in a trancelike coma, was "It is beautiful over there."

BENJAMIN FRANKLIN'S LAST PHILOSOPHIC REMARK

As he lay dying, Ben Franklin's daughter asked him to change his position in the bed. The American statesman, scientist, diplomat, and philosopher said: "A dying man can do nothing easy."

MARIE ANTOINETTE, POLITE TO THE LAST

The last words of Marie Antoinette, the French Queen, were said to her executioner, after she stepped on his foot: "Monsieur, I beg your pardon."

GEORGE BERNARD SHAW'S LAST WORDS

The last words of George Bernard Shaw, the English playwright, were spoken to his nurse as he lay dying: "Sister, you're trying to keep me alive as an old curiosity, but I'm done, I'm finished, I'm going to die."

THE LAST WORDS OF SOCRATES

The last words of the great Greek philosopher, Socrates, as he lay dying were to his friend: "Crito, I owe a cock to Asclepius; will you remember this debt?"

PLATO'S LAST SAYING

Plato, another Greek philosopher and thinker, said as he was getting ready to pass on: "I thank the guiding providence and fortune of my life, first, that I was born a man and a Greek, not a barbarian nor a brute: and next, that I happened to live in the age of Socrates."

THE LAST WORDS OF IBSEN

Henrik Ibsen the Norwegian poet and dramatist died in 1906. When Ibsen's nurse assured his sickbed visitors that he was improving, he replied with what were his last words: "On the contrary."

A SMOKER'S LAST WORDS

U. S. Senator Everett Dirksen of Illinois died soon after an operation for lung cancer in 1969. Among his last words were "They've taken my cigarettes away. . . ."

OSCAR WILDE'S LAST WORDS

"Either this wallpaper goes, or I go."

BILLY THE KID'S LAST WORDS

One of the most legendary outlaws in American history was Billy Bonney, a.k.a. Billy the Kid. Pat Garrett, the newly elected sheriff of Lincoln County, New Mexico, had captured Billy and confined him in an upstairs room over the courthouse. On April 28, 1881, Billy escaped and hid with friendly Hispanic sheepmen on the range around Fort Summer. He even ventured into town for an occasional fandango or more intimate tryst. Sheriff Garrett and his men stole into the town of Fort Sumner on the night of July 14, 1881, thinking that the Kid was somewhere nearby. They inquired but no one would talk. At midnight Garrett slipped into owner of the town Pete Maxwell's bedroom to question him about the Kid. Entirely by coincidence, Billy came into the same bedroom only seconds later, saying " *¿Quien es? ¿Quien es?*" (Who is it? Who is it?). These were Billy's last words. Garrett recognized the voice and fired twice, hitting the Kid in the chest; he dropped to the floor dead.

HENRY DAVID THOREAU'S LAST TWO WORDS

As he was dying the American author last said: "Moose. Indian."

WINSTON CHURCHILL PREDICTS HIS OWN LAST DAY ON EARTH

In 1950 Winston Churchill predicted exactly his last day on earth when he was heard to remark: "Today is the twenty-fourth of January. It is the day my father died. It is the day that I shall die, too." He died on January 24, 1965, fifteen years later to the day.

THE LAST WORDS OF JULIUS CAESAR
"Et tu, Brute?"

A LAST LESSON
On a gravestone in an Edinburgh, Scotland, cemetery: "Beneath this stone a lump of clay/Lies Uncle Peter Dan'els/Who early in the month of May/Took off his winter flannels."

THE LAST QUATRAIN OF NOSTRADAMUS
Michael Nostradamus (1503–1566), French physician and astrologer, acquired a great reputation as a doctor by treating victims of the plague in Europe. He was fascinated by astrology and metaphysics, and in 1555 he wrote a book of more than 900 predictions about the fate of the world. His prophecies are written as four-lined rhymed verses (quatrains) in often cryptic and vague language. Down through the centuries, people have been fascinated by Nostradamus' predictions of the future, and they remain a classic of occult literature. *Centuries*, the title of his book, refers to the contents, which are arranged in sections of 100 verses each. The last prophecy in *Centuries* is: "A great empire will be for England the all-powerful for more than three hundred years, great forces cross by land and sea, the Portuguese will not be pleased."

Last Turns of Phrase

LAST HEIR
In English law, the lord or sovereign to whom lands escheat (revert) for want of an heir.

"LAST" TO A FISHERMAN
A unit of quantity for herring equal to 10,000, 13,200, or 20,000 fish (depending on the size of the fish).

"LAST" TO A FARMER
A unit of weight equal to about 4,000 pounds, or an English unit of capacity for grain equal to 10 quarters or 80 bushels.

LAST CLEAR CHANCE
A doctrine in English and American law regarding negligence. Contributory negligence of the plaintiffs will not bar their action if the defendants had a clear chance of avoiding it.

THE SHOE LAST

A last is a three-dimensional, foot-like part used by shoe manufacturers to form shoes. The name comes from the Old English word "leste" or "laest," which means footprint. The earliest lasts are much older than Old English, which was spoken about 500 to 1100 A.D. Lasts date as far back as 8000 B.C., according to research done by SATRA, the international shoe industry technology center in England.

THE LAST POST

Title of the music played at military burials.

LAST CALL

A bartender's announcement that the customers can order one more drink before the watering hole closes for the eveing.

THE LAST OF THE ROMANS

A title given, at one time or another, to many characters in history, including: Marcus Junius, circa 85–42 B.C., one of the murderers of Julius Caesar; Caius Cassius Longinus, died 42 B.C.; Stilicho (359–408 B.C.), a Vandal and Roman general under Theodosius, who was so dubbed by Procopius; and also Aetius, the general who defended the Gauls against the Franks and other barbarians and defeated Attila near Châlons in 451. François Josephim Terrasse Desbillions, who lived in the eighteenth century, was called the last Roman because of the elegance and purity of his Latin. The Pope called Congreve

Ultimus Romanorum, "the last of the Romans," and the same title was subsequently conferred upon Dr. Johnson, Horace Walpole, and C. J. Fox.

LAST IN FIRST OUT

A method of inventory accounting.

Radio Lasts

THE LAST FRED ALLEN SHOW

Fred Allen was the stage name of John Florence Sullivan, born in Cambridge, Massachusetts, in 1894 and master of the ad-lib. He broadcast his last radio show on June 26, 1949. He and Jack Benny carried a mock feud off and on for thirteen years, the longest-running gag in the history of comedy.

THE GREAT GILDERSLEEVE'S LAST RADIO SHOW

The Great Gildersleeve radio program broadcast its final show in 1958. It began August 31, 1941.

I LOVE A MYSTERY HEROES' LAST NAMES

I Love a Mystery was a radio adventure series featuring heroes Jack, Doc, and Reggie. Their full names were Jack Packard, Doc Long and Reggie York, and they ran the A-1 Detective Agency.

LAST LETTER OF THE RADIO ALPHABET

Words used to differentiate letters in voice transmission over radio are also called the phonetic alphabet. Last letter of current radio alphabet: Zulu. Last letter of radio alphabet used during World War II: Zebra.

Amos 'n' Andy's Last Names

Amos Jones and Andrew H. Brown. The last time the very popular *Amos 'n' Andy* show ran was in 1943. The show was canceled after fifteen years when Campbell Soup, whose sales were cut in half because of the wartime tin shortages, could no longer sponsor the show.

Fay and Evey's Last Name

Perkins. They were the daughters in the Ma Perkins radio show.

Ichabod's Last Name

Mudd. In the radio series *Captain Midnight*, Ichabod was Captain Midnight's mechanic.

Amelia Earhart's Last Contact with the Coast Guard

The last radio communication Amelia Earhart had was on July 3, 1937, with the Coast Guard cutter U.S.S. *Itasca*. Her call sign was KHAQQ.

Last Name of Lord Haw Haw

Joyce. Born in Brooklyn in 1906, William Joyce was taken to England as a child. He moved to Germany just before the start of World War II and broadcast Nazi propaganda in English throughout the war. He was captured by the British in 1945. Despite his American birth, Joyce was judged subject to

British jurisdiction because he held a British passport. He was convicted of treason and hanged.

THE LAST TUTANKHAMEN TOOT

King Tutankhamen's 22 1/2-inch trumpet of silver and gold, as well as his 19 1/2-inch copper trumpet, were last heard on a world radio broadcast in 1939, after 3,297 years of silence.

THE LAST LONE RANGER

The Lone Ranger was originally created for radio by George W. Trendle and was written by Fran Striker. It first aired in Detroit, Michigan, on radio station WXYZ. The voice of the Lone Ranger was provided by Jack Deeds, who was replaced by George Seaton, who in turn was replaced by Earle Grazer. Grazer's voice was perfect, but unfortunately he was killed in an automobile accident. Brace Beemer became the voice of the Lone Ranger until it last aired May 27, 1955, on the ABC Network. In the meantime, the Lone Ranger had moved into television as well.

The Lasts of Crime and Punishment

JIMMY HOFFA'S LAST PHONE CALL TO HIS WIFE

The last time Jimmy Hoffa's wife heard from him was 2:30 P.M. July 30, 1975. He called from the Machus Red Fox restaurant in Bloomfield Township, fifteen miles northwest of Detroit, and said he had been stood up.

THE LAST SURVIVING WITNESS OF LINCOLN'S MURDER

As a child of five, Samuel James Seymor heard the shot, saw the president slump forward, and watched the assassin jump to the stage. Seymor, who was born in 1860 and died April 13,

1956, was the last known witness to the assassination of Abraham Lincoln.

LAST PUBLIC EXECUTION BY GUILLOTINE

The last person to be executed by guillotine in public was murderer Eugen Weidmann, who died before a large crowd in Versailles, France, 4:50 P.M., June 17, 1939.

LAST EXECUTION BY GUILLOTINE

The last nonpublic use of the guillotine was the September 10, 1977, execution of torturer and murderer Hamida Djandoubi at Baumetes Prison, Marseilles, France. France abolished capital punishment on September 9, 1981.

DEVIL'S ISLAND'S LAST DAY AS A PENAL COLONY

The dreaded French penal colony was closed on August 22, 1953. It was founded in 1852, off the coast of French Guiana in South America. Its most famous political prisoner was Major Alfred Dreyfus. Henri Charriere, one of the few prisoners to escape Devil's Island, wrote a best-selling book, *Papillon*, about the hell on earth that was life on Devil's Island.

THE LAST OF ALCATRAZ PRISON

Alcatraz Federal Prison was closed in March of 1963. An island in San Francisco Bay, Alcatraz was named by the Spanish for its large pelican population. The facility served as a United States military prison from 1859 to 1933 and a federal prison from 1933. In October of 1972 it became part of the National Parks Service's Goldengate Recreation Area.

THE LAST DAYS OF AL CAPONE

On January 25, 1947, Gangster Al "Scarface" Capone died of general paresis, the devastating final stage of syphilis. In the 1920s, Capone controlled the Chicago underworld and the bootleg wars. He probably ordered more than 300 murders and eluded prosecution until 1932, when federal agents nailed him for tax evasion. Capone was paroled in 1939 for health reasons and died the same year in Miami, Florida.

LAST TIME THE LINDBERGH BABY WAS SEEN ALIVE

On Tuesday, March 1, 1931, at the Lindbergh estate, Highfields, Anne Lindbergh had put twenty-month-old Charlie to bed about 7 P.M. Betty, the nursemaid, checked on him at 8 P.M.; he was sleeping peacefully, but when she returned to check on him at 9:30 P.M., he was gone. She was the last known person to see the Lindbergh baby alive. On May 12, 1931, a truck driver found the infant's body on the edge of Princeton Road, in Hopewell, New Jersey.

LAST MOMENTS OF PROHIBITION

The 1919 Volstead Act, which outlawed the production, sale, and transportation of alcohol in the United States, officially ended at 3:32 P.M. Mountain Standard Time, on December 5, 1933.

BONNIE AND CLYDE'S LAST CAR

On April 29, 1934, the outlaws Bonnie Parker and Clyde Barrow stole their last car, an almost new gray Ford V-8 with bumper guards and a hot water heater, from Jesse Warren, a roof contractor in Topeka, Kansas. Over the next twenty-three days Bonnie and Clyde drove 7,500 miles before being ambushed by Texas Rangers in Louisiana.

LAST WOMAN HANGED IN ENGLAND

The execution of Ruth Ellis by hanging in 1955 led to the suspension of capital punishment throughout England.

THE LAST TIME WITCHCRAFT WAS PUNISHED IN ENGLAND

The last punishment for the crime of practicing witchcraft in England was administered on October 29, 1808.

THE LAST NAVY MAN HANGED FOR MUTINY

The last U.S. Navy man hanged for mutiny was the son of Secretary of War John C. Spencer. In 1842, Midshipman Philip Spencer was found guilty, along with two enlisted men, of scheming to turn their ship, the U.S.S. *Somers*, to piracy.

D. B. COOPER LAST SEEN

Last seen on November 25, 1971, D. B. Cooper, the skyjacker, collected $200,000 in ransom money, parachuted from Northwest 727 jet Flight 305, and vanished, never to be seen again.

THE JAMES GANG'S LAST TRAIN ROBBERY

The last train robbery of Jesse and his brother Frank, along with Charles Ford, Dick Liddel, Clarence Rite, and Wood Rite, was the Chicago–Alton Express Train. The robbers took $1,500 in cash, along with gold and jewels, on August 7, 1881.

THE LAST PERSON KILLED BY BILLY THE KID

The last person Billy the Kid killed was the warden of the Messilla, New Mexico, jail, Robert W. Ollinger. The Kid shotgunned the warden and escaped on April 28, 1881.

WILD BILL HICKOK'S LAST HAND

The last poker hand held by gambler Wild Bill Hickok was a full house of aces and eights, now known as "the dead man's hand." He was shot and killed by Jack McCall in Deadwood, Dakota Territory, on August 2, 1876.

DUTCH SCHULTZ'S LAST NAME

Gangster Dutch Schultz's real full name was Arthur Flegenheimer. Dutch's last words were a meaningless babble that included two immortal ravings: "A boy who never wept nor dashed a thousand kim," and "Mother is the best bet, and don't let Satan draw you too fast."

THE LAST PERSON BURNED AT THE STAKE IN GREAT BRITAIN

According to J. F. Sutton's *Annals of Crime*, published in 1859, thirty-year-old Phoebe Harrius was the last person burned at the stake—in front of Newgate Prison a few days after being sentenced at the Old Bailey on July 21, 1786, for coining false money, which was then classed as high treason.

COLUMBUS'S LAST TRIP TO THE NEW WORLD

Among Columbus's first landfalls in 1492 was Hispaniola (Espaniola), the second largest island of the West Indies, which lies between Cuba and Puerto Rico. (Today it is occupied by Haiti and the Dominican Republic.) In 1493, with seventeen ships and 1,500 colonists, he returned to Hispaniola to find that his first colony had been destroyed by the natives. He founded a new colony, but discipline and organization were difficult. In 1498, he came back to Hispaniola, this time with convicts to serve as colonists. Discipline got even worse. Reports of wretched conditions in the colony led Ferdinand and Isabella to send an independent governor in 1500. The governor sent Columbus back to Spain in chains.

THE LAST MUTINEERS OF THE BOUNTY

In 1790 Fletcher Christian, some Tahitian women, and part of the mutinous crew of H.M.S. *Bounty* took refuge on Pitcairn Island, a lovely volcanic island in the South Pacific, and founded a colony. Eighteen years later, when a ship landed on the island, they found John Adams, the last surviving crew member of the *Bounty*, and twenty-three women and children. Their descendants continue to live at the island colony. Mr. Christian was never found.

THE LAST MEAL OF THE MAN WHO DINED MEN TO DEATH

French murderer Père Gourier was responsible for the deaths of seven to nine men during the reign of King Louis XIV, the Sun King.

Gourier, a rich landowner, chose a victim each year and simply wined and dined him to death, using no poisons or anything illegal. His method was to gorge his guests with rich, heavy food, not once, but at every meal, and every day, for as long as it took. Since the food was free, his victims happily obliged by stuffing themselves. Waiters at the expensive Parisian restaurants knew Gourier well, and soon discovered his taste for murder, but they could do nothing about it.

Gourier's last victim was named Ameline, and was the second assistant to the public executioner, a fact that no doubt amused Gourier. But Ameline had an appetite even greater than his benefactor. Those who watched this Frenchman eat swore he had hollow legs. Gourier feted him for one year, then another. Ameline looked healthier than ever, so Gourier ordered only the heaviest of dishes, food even he had trouble digesting. He was determined to kill Ameline, even if it depleted his entire fortune. Ameline, however, was on to him, perhaps due to a warning from a waiter, and he would periodically disappear for two or three days at a time to purge his body with castor oil and laxatives. Gourier never suspected a thing.

One night, at Paris's most expensive restaurant, Gourier turned red, then white, when served his fourteenth slice of sirloin steak (in an effort to keep up with his dinner companion, Ameline). Gourier threw his head back, then slumped forward and died. While he never made it to the last course, many felt he had received his just desserts.

THE LAST OF MIRANDA

If you have ever watched TV or the movies, you've seen law officers, at the moment of arrest, read the suspect his or her Miranda rights. Those rights derive from the case of Ernesto

Miranda, who abducted and raped a young girl and, because of his prior record, was picked up and identified by the victim. Miranda made a written confession of the crime and said that he had been informed of his rights. A court-appointed attorney argued that he had not been informed of his right to legal counsel. The case went all the way to the Supreme Court, which by a narrow margin ruled in favor of Miranda, saying that a criminal suspect must be told of his right to silence, that his remarks may be held against him, and that he has a right to counsel during interrogation, even if he could not afford one. On the basis of new evidence Miranda was again convicted of the same crime, imprisoned, and eventually paroled. Ernesto Miranda met his demise at the wrong end of a knife in a barroom brawl.

MATA HARI'S LAST REQUEST

Mata Hari (Margaretha Zeller) was a Dutch dancer working in Paris who joined the German Secret Service in 1907. During World War I she betrayed important military secrets confided in her by high-ranking Allied officers with whom she was intimate. She was tried by the French government and condemned to death. Mata Hari was awakened at 4 A.M. on October 15, 1917, and prepared for the firing squad. All the fantastic plans made for her escape by her numerous lovers had failed. Mata Hari made one last request: permission to write three last letters, one of which was to her daughter Banda, from whom she asked forgiveness. Ironically, beautiful Banda became a spy herself and eventually met the same fate as her mother.

JACK THE RIPPER'S LAST VICTIM

Although as many as fourteen murders were at one time attributed Jack the Ripper, it is generally agreed that only five were actually committed by his hand. Mary Ann Nichols, Annie Chapman, Elizabeth Stride, and Catherine Eddowes were his first four victims. His last victim, Mary Jane Kelly, was found dead on November 9, 1888, on a blood-soaked mattress in her room in a small East End tenement. After this murder, Jack the Ripper vanished.

LAST WITCHES HANGED IN SALEM

On September 22, 1692, in the Massachusetts Bay Colony town of Salem, eight people accused of witchcraft were hanged in the center of town, six women and two men. They were Mary Easty, Martha Corey, Alice Parker, Anne Poutador, Mary Parker, Wilmot Reed, Samuel Wardwell, and Mary Scott.

DR. MUDD'S LAST YEAR IN PRISON

Dr. Samuel Mudd was sentenced to life in prison for conspiracy in President Lincoln's assassination. He was kept in chains at Fort Jefferson military prison on Dry Tortugas, Florida, because of an attempt to escape. During a yellow fever epidemic he saved the lives of many guards and prisoners, and was pardoned in 1869 by President Andrew Johnson.

THE LAST ROMAN VICTIM OF GOLDEN THROAT

Marcus Licinius Crassus, a Roman financier, politician, and notorious moneylender, died in 53 B.C. when Parthian soldiers poured molten gold down his throat.

The Last of Their Kind

THE LAST OF THE AUKS

The flightless great auk, *Pinguinus impennis* or gare fowl, was the largest of the great auks, swimming and diving birds once common to the North Atlantic. About the size of a goose, black above and grayish-white below, the flight-less great auk was easily slaughtered in its breeding grounds for its flesh, feathers, and oil. The last auks were seen in 1844.

THE LAST CAROLINA PARAKEET

The last known Carolina parakeets were sighted on Lake Okee-chobee in 1904 by ornithologist Dr. Frank Chapman.

THE LAST LABRADOR DUCK

The last Labrador duck died on December 12, 1872.

THE LAST OF THE HEATH HEN

The species became extinct when the last heath hen disappeared on March 11, 1932.

THE LAST PASSENGER PIGEON

The last passenger pigeon, *Ctopistes migratorius*, died in captivity in the Cincinnati Zoo on September 1, 1914. The bird's name was Martha. Passenger pigeons were among the most frequently seen birds in America. In the fall the pigeons went south in large swarms. Amateur and professional hunters contributed to their extinction. After 1880 the swarms became thinner and rarer, and by 1906 the birds had completely disappeared.

THE LAST WILD DONKEY

The onager, a wild donkey, *Equus hemiomus onage*, which lived in Syria and was hunted for meat, became extinct in 1927.

LAST STELLER'S SEA COW

The last Steller's sea cows, *Hydramalis gigas stelleri*, died on one of the Bering Islands in 1768. They were hunted for their meat and fat.

THE LAST DODO

This flightless swan-sized bird, which weighed about 25 kilos and lived on the Indian Ocean islands of Mauritius and Reunion, was last seen in 1681. Another source claims they also lived on Rodrigues Island, near the above two, and were last seen there in 1850. The Dutch called the dodo the "nauseous bird" because no manner of cooking would make it palatable. Perhaps the most famous Dodo is the one in *Alice in Wonderland*.

THE LAST OF THE DINOSAURS
Archosauria, "ruling reptiles," is a class of reptiles that included dinosaurs, pterosaurs, and crocodiles. The first two disappeared about 65 million years ago.

THE LAST CALIFORNIA CONDORS
The last of the California condors is flying around and pretty lonely—since there is only one left in the wild. There is hope that a chick hatched in the San Diego Zoo will eventually be released.

THE LAST CUBAN RED MACAW
The Cuban Red Macaw disappeared from Cuba in 1894.

THE LAST JAMAICAN IGUANA
The Jamaican iguana was last seen in Jamaica in 1894.

THE LAST GRIZZLY BEAR IN CALIFORNIA
Though it is the central figure in the state's flag, the last grizzly bear in California was spotted in the Sierras in 1924.

THE LAST OF THE TRILOBITES
The last of the trilobites disappeared 230 million years ago. Trilobites were the first animals to have eyes. Human beings

have one lens in each eye, but some trilobites had as many as 20,000. Over 10,000 species are known. They appeared 570 million years ago and are the ancestors of today's shrimps and lobsters.

THE LAST GUADALUPE ISLAND CARACARA

The last Guadalupe Island caracara, a long-legged falcon, died on December 1, 1900.

The Lasts of Coins,
Stamps, Stocks and Money

THE LAST BALANCED BUDGET
The U.S. budget was last balanced in the 1960 fiscal year. Receipts for that year were $77.763 trillion and outlays totaled $76.539 trillion.

THE LAST STABLE ECONOMIC DECADE IN U.S. HISTORY
The Roaring 1920s. During that decade, federal receipts average $41.9 trillion per year, while outlays averaged $33.8 trillion. By the time of World War II, that ratio had reversed itself to the point where the nation was annually spending 2.5 times more than its income.

THE LAST YEAR THERE WERE FEWER THAN
100,000 BANKRUPTCIES IN THE UNITED STATES
1985.

LAST TIME THE UNITED STATES HAD NO NATIONAL DEBT

Between the years 1835 and 1837 the United States of America had no national debt.

THE LAST FIVE-CENT CALL

The last time a telephone call cost five cents was November 9, 1951. The next day New York and other large American cities doubled the cost to ten cents.

THE LAST $500 BILL

Bills in denominations of $500 and up (including $1,000, $5,000, and $10,000) were last printed in 1969. Bills from the previous print, in 1945, had satisfied demand for twenty-four years. Today the highest denomination printed is the $100 bill.

THE LAST INDIAN HEAD NICKELS MINTED

The last Indian Head or Buffalo nickel was issued in 1938 by the Denver Mint. Over 7 million were struck. James Frazer used three men as models to design the Indian head: Two Moons, Crow Tails, and John Big Tail. The buffalo was modeled after Black Diamond of the New York Zoological Gardens. The Indian Head nickel was first issued in 1913.

THE LAST THREE-CENT COIN

The last three-cent pieces (75 percent copper and 25 percent nickel) were issued in 1889. Nearly 22,000 were struck for circulation and 3,436 were struck as proof coins (not intended for circulation).

THE LAST LINCOLN WHEAT CENT

The last Lincoln cent with wheat ears on the reverse side was issued in 1958. 1,054,353,952 coins were minted in both the Philadelphia and San Francisco mints.

THE LAST UNITED STATES BUDGET SURPLUS

The last time the United States had a budget surplus was June 22, 1836. The twenty-six states divided the extra $928 million.

THE LAST TIME RED WAS IN THE BLACK

The last time red meant you were in the black was 1300 B.C. in China. The Chinese wrote positive numbers in red and negative numbers in black—the opposite of today's western accounting systems.

THE LAST TIME UNITED STATES GOLD COINS WERE CIRCULATED

Gold coins were last circulated in 1933. In 1934 the United States abandoned the gold standard. The Gold Reserve Act of 1934 stipulated that gold could not be used as a medium of domestic exchange, and made it illegal for private persons or firms to own gold bullion.

THE LAST TIME QUARTERS AND DIMES ACTUALLY CONTAINED SILVER

The last time United States quarters and dimes actually had any silver content was 1964. In 1965 the U.S. Treasury ceased to put silver in the 10- and 25-cent coins. At the same time they reduced the silver content in half-dollars from 90 percent to 40 percent.

THE LAST TIME THE UNITED STATES HAD MONEY TO BURN

Used paper money eventually becomes so worn that it has to be destroyed by the Federal Reserve Banks. Since 1963, anti-pollution laws have forbidden the incineration of worn bills. Instead, used paper money may be shredded for confetti, molded into artificial logs, used to lubricate oil drills, or plowed under as landfill. You can buy stationery made of recycled paper money from the Crane Company, which makes the paper for the United States mint.

THE LAST UNITED STATES PENNY POST CARD

The last time post cards could be mailed for one cent was in 1951. In 1952 the cost of mailing a post card doubled to two cents.

THE LAST £2 COIN ISSUED

The £2 coin in Great Britain was issued in 1989 to commemorate the (British) Bill of Rights and the Scottish Claim of Rights. Nearly 5 million coins were minted. Although they are legal tender, they were never intended for general circulation.

THE LAST DAYS OF CHANGE ONLY

The last time America used coins exclusively was on February 2, 1690. The next day the first paper money was issued by Massachusetts to pay soldiers who had served in a campaign.

THE LAST PERSON TO MAKE $2.5 MILLION ON A SHOESTRING

Harvey Kennedy invented and patented the shoelace in September of 1856 and made $2.5 million as a result.

THE LAST POLL TAX

The last poll tax was collected in the United States in 1963. When the Twenty-fourth Amendment to the Constitution was adopted in 1964, the poll tax was abolished. The poll tax had been used by many states to keep poor blacks from voting.

THE LAST TIME FOUR CAME UP SEVEN TIMES IN ROULETTE

Croupier Liz Harlow-Smith of the Stakis Club in Bristol, England, was the last person in the world to spin the roulette wheel seven times and have the ball land on the black four each time. It's a 100 billion–to–one chance, according to statisticians. If a bettor had placed £10 on four and let the winnings ride, the winnings would have ended up at £949 billion, house limits and bank permitting. The record spinning took place September 1993.

THE LAST UNITED STATES INDIAN HEAD PENNY

The last Indian Head penny was minted in 1909. In Philadelphia, 14,370,645 were minted, and in San Francisco, 309,000.

THE LAST TWENTY-DOLLAR WHITE HOUSE RENOVATION

In 1948, the U.S. Treasury's Bureau of Engraving and Printing changed the design on the back of the twenty-dollar bill, updating the White House illustration to conform with several major structural changes made to the White House during the Truman presidency. The changes were the addition of a balcony on the front portico, and two more chimneys. The word "The" was also added to "White House" just below the illustration.

Last Names

CHER'S LAST NAME

Cher's full name is Cherilyn Sarkisian.

YES, SANTA, VIRGINIA HAS A LAST NAME

O'Hanlon was the last name of the eight-year-old girl named Virginia who wrote to the *New York Sun*, asking if there really was a Santa Claus.

AGATHA CHRISTIE'S LAST NAME

Mallowan. Her full name was Dame Agatha Mary Clarissa Miller Christie Mallowan.

TARZAN'S LAST NAME

John Clayton, Jr., Lord Greystoke, was the childhood name of Tarzan.

BOB DYLAN'S REAL LAST NAME

Zimmerman.

THE MOST POPULAR LAST NAMES

CHINA: Chang. FRANCE: Martin. GERMANY: Schultz. GREAT BRITAIN: Smith. KOREA: Kim. HOLLAND: De Vries. RUSSIA: Ivanov. SPAIN: Garcia. SWEDEN: Johannson. U.S.A.: Smith.

LI'L ABNER'S LAST NAME

Yokum. Li'l Abner was the hillbilly for whom Al Capp's comic strip was named.

RICK'S LAST NAME

The last name of the character named Rick, played by Humphrey Bogart in the 1942 movie classic *Casablanca*, was Blaine.

THE LONE RANGER'S LAST NAME

The secret identity of the Texas Ranger known as the Lone Ranger was John Reid.

ALICE IN WONDERLAND'S LAST NAME

In the novel *Alice's Adventures in Wonderland*, written in 1865 by Lewis Carroll, Alice does not have a last name. However, the book was written in honor of Carroll's young friend, Alice Liddell.

LAST NAME OF *FATHER KNOWS BEST*

The last name of the family in the TV series *Father Knows Best*, starring Robert Young and Jane Wyatt, was Anderson.

TOKYO ROSE'S LAST NAME

D'Aquino. Iva Ikuko Toguri d'Aquino spoke in a bright and sexy voice, broadcasting Japanese propaganda about Japan's successes in order to demoralize the Allied troops in the Pacific theater during World War II. She was an American citizen with Japanese parents. She had a degree from UCLA, and had been visiting a sick relative in Japan when war broke out. She chose to join the Japanese Broadcasting Company and was trained by an American prisoner of war. In 1948 she was tried by the United States and sentenced to ten years in prison and fined $10,000 for treason.

DIAMOND JIM'S LAST NAME

The last name of the New York financier nicknamed Diamond Jim was Brady (James Buchanan Brady).

LAST NAME OF THE RED BARON

Richthofen. Manfred von Richthofen, the German flying ace, nicknamed the Red Baron, is credited with shooting down eighty enemy aircraft, the highest total of any flier in World War I. He was killed in action on April 21, 1918.

HAWKEYE'S LAST NAME

In the popular television series *M*A*S*H*, which ran on CBS from 1972 to 1983, Hawkeye's last name was Pierce (Benjamin Franklin Pierce). The role was played by Alan Alda.

LUCY'S MAIDEN NAME

In the popular TV comedy series *I Love Lucy*, Lucy's last name before she married Ricky Ricardo was McGillicuddy.

THE LAST NAME OF BIG POISON AND LITTLE POISON

Waner. The two brothers played the outfield for the Pittsburgh
Pirates in the 1920s and 1930s. Paul was known as Big Poison. He led the National League in batting three times, and
Lloyd, known as Little Poison, had a lifetime batting average of
over .300.

CALAMITY JANE'S LAST NAME

Canary. Martha Jane Canary. The name is disputed but most
sources say Canary. This character of the American frontier
was born in Princeton, Missouri, in 1852. The origin of her
nickname is obscure. She was an expert marksman, and
claimed to have been a Pony Express rider and a scout for
Custer; she appeared at the Pan-American Exposition in Buffalo, New York. She died in poverty in 1903 and is buried beside Wild Bill Hickok in Deadwood, South Dakota.

BABY RUTH'S LAST NAME

Contrary to popular belief, the Baby Ruth candy bar was not
named after Babe Ruth. Baby Ruth's last name was Cleveland;
the candy bar was named after the oldest daughter of President Grover Cleveland, born in 1891.

McGUFFEY WAS HIS LAST NAME

An American college teacher, William Holmes McGuffey, wrote
his first readers in 1836. The schoolbooks, known as McGuffey
Readers, have sold over 122 million copies.

TYPHOID MARY'S LAST NAME

Mallon. Mary Mallon was an institutional and household cook who spread the disease typhoid from house to house in the early part of the twentieth century. She died in 1938.

MALCOLM X'S LAST NAME

Little. The black activist took the name Malik El Shabazz when he joined the Black Muslims. Later a pilgrimage to Mecca earned him the title El-Haji.

MADONNA'S LAST NAME

This controversial performer, actress, and singer was born in Bay City, Michigan, August 16, 1958, and named Madonna Louise Veronica Ciccone.

JOHN WAYNE'S REAL LAST NAME

John Wayne's real last name was Morrison. The Duke's full name at birth was Marion Michael Morrison.

AGATHA CHRISTIE'S ROMANTIC NOM DE PLUME

The nom de plume under which Agatha Christie wrote romantic novels was Mary Westmacott.

ANN-MARGRET'S LAST NAME

The first-name-only actress, singer, dancer, and entertainer Ann-Margret's last name is Olsson. She was born in Valsjobyn, Sweden, on April 28, 1941.

TWIGGY'S LAST NAME

The very thin, very popular 1960s English model Twiggy was born Leslie Hornby.

MINNESOTA FATS' LAST NAME

The legendary pool hustler Minnesota Fats grew up in the Washington Heights section of New York City as Rudolph Wanderone, Jr.

REMBRANDT'S LAST NAME

The last name of the Dutch painter and etcher is van Rijn (or Ryn). He lived and painted in the seventeenth century, and his full name is Rembrandt Harmenszoon van Rijn.

BARBIE DOLL'S LAST NAME

Barbie Doll's official last name is Roberts. She was named for Barbie Handler, the daughter of the cofounders of Mattel, Ruth and Elliott Handler. They founded Mattel with Harold Mattson in 1945. Barbie was patented in 1953.

DOROTHY'S LAST NAME

The full name of the little girl swept into adventure by a Kansas tornado in *The Wizard of Oz* is Dorothy Gale.

The Lasts of Planes,
Trains and Automobiles

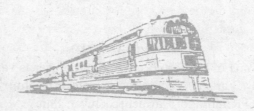

THE LAST MODEL T FORD

The last Model T Ford came off the production line on May 26, 1927. Like its more than 15 million predecessors, number 15,007,033 was black in color.

THE LAST DESIGN OF DR. PORSCHE

The 1550 Silver Spyder Porsche was the last car designed by Dr. Ferdinand Porsche (1875–1951), who also designed the car that Hitler called the Volkswagen ("the people's car").

THE LAST TUCKER CAR

The last of the fifty-one Tucker automobiles ever produced was made in 1948. Preston Tucker's dream car was truly ahead of its time—219 inches long but only 60 inches high, low for automobiles of the day. All independent suspension and rear-mounted flat-six engine. A fully sealed water-cooling system—an industry first. It had a central "cyclops-eye" headlight that turned with the wheels. Doors were cut into the roof to ease entry and exit. The windshield glass popped out harmlessly on impact, and there was a "safety chamber" where passengers could dive in case of impending collision. Tucker was taken to court by the Securities Exchange Commission on allegations of stock fraud. Though he was exonerated in 1950, it was too late to resurrect the Tucker car. Of the fifty-one Tuckers built, forty-nine survive.

THE LAST STATE TO ISSUE PHOTO DRIVER'S LICENSES
In 1984 New York became the last state in the nation to put photographs on driver's licenses.

THE LAST PACKARD
The Studebaker-Packard Co. made the last Packard on August 19, 1958.

THE LAST VULCAN FLYING BOMBER
The last Vulcan bomber was purchased in 1993 by the Walton family, who run their own aviation museum near Lutterworth, Leicestershire, England. The sale marked the end of the Vulcan's thirty-seven years of service with the RAF. The Vulcan was originally part of Britain's V-Bomber nuclear deterrent force.

THE LAST OF THE L-29 CORD AUTOMOBILES
The Cord, a rakish, altogether beautiful, and ahead-of-its-time design, was the first front-wheel-drive car. The Auburn Auto-

mobile Company of Auburn, Indiana, introduced the Model L-29 in November of 1929. The introduction coincided with the stock market crash. In early 1931, prices were reduced to $2,395 from $2,595 to increase sales, but to little avail. The last of the original Cords rolled off the assembly line in early 1932 after some 4,429 cars had been built.

THE LAST HORNET

The Hudson Hornet was the last of the Hudson cars made. In 1957 only 1,345 of the 3,876 cars manufactured were sold, and American Motors discontinued the line.

THE LAST FLIGHT OF PAN AM AIRLINES

Pan American Airlines met its demise on December 3, 1991, when Delta Airlines told the bankruptcy court that it would not put any more money into Pan Am, effectively shutting down the airline. There may have been a flight in progress on December 4 when the shut-down order went into effect.

THE LAST FLIGHT OF THE SPRUCE GOOSE

The all-wood eight-engine flying boat, built by the eccentric billionaire Howard Hughes, was the ultimate wealthy man's toy. Hughes built the huge wooden plane, which he named *Hercules*, for the war effort, but the war was over by the time it was ready for a test flight. It was lumbering, difficult to camouflage, highly inflammable, and would have been a sitting duck for any German or Japanese pilot. It held a great fascination for the public. On November 2, 1947, Hughes took the controls and a group of reporters on the maiden flight of the

Spruce Goose, a name given the giant plane by the press and detested by Hughes. The first flight was a short trip of a mile at 45 mph, and its second and last flight was another mile at 90 mph. Hughes promised more flights but they never took place.

THE LAST WOODEN TRAIN TO BROOKLYN

The last wooden passenger train car of the New York City subway system was taken out of service in 1969.

THE LAST EDSEL

The Edsel was one of the biggest flops in automobile history. The Ford Motor Company first conceived the Edsel in 1954 when the demand for a medium-priced car was strong. By the time the cars were introduced in 1957, however, the market had changed. Also, the radical vertical grille of the Corsair model was startlingly different and not appealing to the automobile-buying public. By the time the last Edsels were produced in 1959 (the 1960 model), Ford had lost $250 million.

LAST NAME OF AUTOMOBILE-BUILDING BROTHERS HORACE AND JOHN

Dodge.

LAST NAME OF AUTOMOBILE-BUILDING BROTHERS AUGUST AND FREDERICK S.

Duesenberg.

Last Name of Gaston and Louis, Automobile Makers

Chevrolet.

The Last Stanley Steamer

The Stanley brothers of Massachusetts produced steam-driven automobiles from 1897 until the last Stanley Steamer, as they were called, was built just after World War II.

The Last Flight of the *Hindenburg*

The last flight of the German lighter-than-air ship ended at 7 P.M., May 6, 1937, when thirty-six passengers and crew members died as the dirigible burst into flames while approaching the landing mast at Lakehurst, New Jersey.

Last Flight out of Vietnam

On April 4, 1975, World Airways 727 was the last flight out of Da Nang Air Base at the end of the Vietnam War. It was the final rescue mission to evacuate United States personnel and supporters before the North Vietnamese and Viet Cong took control of South Vietnam. Ed Daly, then World Airways chief executive, was at the controls on that fateful day.

Amelia Earhart's Last Letter

The last letter to her husband before her last flight: "Please know that I am quite aware of the hazards. Women must try to do things as men have tried. When they fail, their failure must be but a challenge to others."

THE LAST AMERICAN DIRIGIBLE

After fifty-five years at the bottom of the sea, the 785-foot-long *Macon*, the last surviving United States dirigible, was found in 1,500 feet of chilly waters 45 miles south of San Francisco in 1990.

The End of the Line

THE LAST KING OF BABYLON
Belshazzar was the last king of Babylon.

THE LAST KING OF FRANCE
The last King of France, Louis Philippe (1773–1850), the citizen king in the Bourbon–Orléans line, reigned from 1830 to 1848. The monarchy of Louis Philippe was established in the July Revolution of 1830. Initially welcomed by business and professional classes, the new ruler eventually lost favor as his government slid into corruption, subversion of parliamentary power, suppression of civil liberties, and economic mismanagement. The February Revolution of 1848 dislodged Louis Philippe and established the Second Republic.

THE LAST KING OF PRUSSIA
William I (born 1797) was the last king of Prussia. He reigned from 1861 to 1871, when he became Emperor of Germany.

THE LAST CZAR OF RUSSIA

On March 15, 1917, after the Kerenski revolution, Nicholas II abdicated the throne to which he had ascended on October 20, 1894. In July 1918, after the Bolsheviks seized power, he was murdered along with his entire family.

TUTANKHAMEN: THE LAST OF HIS DYNASTY

Pharaoh of Egypt for nine years, King Tut was the last of his dynasty. He died in 137 B.C. Although he was a relatively obscure monarch, he is known because of Howard Carter's discovery of his tomb, intact. All other royal tombs had been ransacked in antiquity. Tutankhamen became pharaoh when he was about nine years old. After he died, his widow was to have married a Hittite prince, but the prince was killed on his trip to Egypt.

THE LAST DAY OF EDWARD VIII'S REIGN

On December 11, 1937, Edward VIII of England, the Uncrowned King, abdicated, ending a 325-day reign. He was the first English monarch to relinquish his throne voluntarily. His brother, next oldest in line, became King George VI. The ex-king was granted the title of "Duke of Windsor" and on June 3, 1937, made Wallis Warfield Simpson, an American, his Duchess.

THE LAST ROYAL GOVERNOR OF NEW JERSEY

The last Royal Governor of New Jersey was William Franklin, illegitimate son of Benjamin Franklin.

NAPOLEON'S LAST ADDRESS

His last residence was on Saint Helena, an island in the South
Atlantic 1,200 miles west of Africa, where he had been exiled
in 1815. He died there in 1821.

THE LAST AZTEC EMPEROR

The last Aztec emperor was Montezuma II, who reigned from
1502 to 1520. In 1519 the Spanish conquistador Hernando
Cortés landed in Mexico. At first Montezuma was unsure
whether the Spaniards were gods or men, and became convinced that they were gods. He allowed Cortés to enter the island capital of Tenochtitlan without a battle, and the Aztec
emperor was taken prisoner. The sheer brutality of the Spanish invaders aroused the anger of the Aztec city's inhabitants,
and during the ensuing battle, Montezuma II died under mys-
terious circumstances.

LAST REIGNING QUEEN OF SCOTLAND

Mary Queen of Scots, the last queen of Scotland, alienated
even some of her closest supporters when she married the earl
of Bothwell. The queen was imprisoned at Lochleven Castle
and, on July 24, 1567, she abdicated in favor of her son, who
became King James VI of Scotland. With help from a few brave
friends, Mary escaped and decided to leave Scotland and go to
England to beg support from her cousin Elizabeth. She never
returned to Scotland. Elizabeth incarcerated her for nineteen
years. Mary was found guilty of complicity in a plot to assassi-
nate Elizabeth and was sentenced to death. On February 8,
1587, she was beheaded and buried at Peterborough. When

her son James ascended the English throne, he had her interred in Westminster Abbey.

LAST SHAH OF IRAN

In 1979 Muhammad Reza Shah Pahlavi became the last Shah of Iran when he was deposed, and the country was declared an Islamic republic after more than 2,500 years as an independent monarchy.

THE LAST KING OF EGYPT

On July 23, 1952, the military overthrew the corrupt government of King Farouk. Although he never reigned, his seven-month-old son succeeded him and became the last king of Egypt.

THE LAST KING AND QUEEN OF HAWAII

In 1875, Kalakaua, the king of Hawaii (1874–1891), signed a treaty with the United States permitting easy access to American markets for Hawaiian sugarcane. Kalakaua attempted to increase the powers of the monarchy, and, partly in reaction, his successor, Liliuokalani, the queen of Hawaii, was deposed in 1893, primarily by foreign businesspersons who established a Republic of Hawaii the following year. On August 12, 1898, the United States annexed Hawaii, and in 1959, Hawaii became a state, the last to be admitted to the union.

THE LAST KING OF ROMANIA

On December 30, 1947, the Romanians forced young King Michael, the last reigning monarch in Eastern Europe, from the throne and established a People's Republic, with a constitution modeled after the Soviet Union's. King Michael, an aeronautical engineer, lives in Switzerland with his wife and nine daughters.

ITALY'S LAST KING

In May 1946 the third king of all Italy, Victor Emmanuel III, abdicated in favor of his son, Humbert II, in a belated effort to save the monarchy. Just one month later, the Italian people overwhelmingly voted for a republican form of government. In June of 1946, Humbert II (whose reign was just that one month) went into exile in Portugal.

THE LAST RULER OF THE UNITED ROMAN EMPIRE

Theodosius I (the Great) was appointed ruler of the east by Gratian (Roman emperor of the West); he later became sole emperor and the last ruler of the united (East and West) Roman empire from 395 to 392 B.C. Upon his death, the Roman Empire reverted into two parts, East and West.

THE LAST ATTEMPT TO SAVE MARIE ANTOINETTE FROM THE GUILLOTINE

Although there were many attempts to rescue Marie Antoinette from the guillotine, the last one came on August 28, 1793. She was being held at the Conciergerie in Paris when the Chevalier de Rougeville, a nobleman who was willing to risk his life to save her, entered her cell with the inspector, who was a secret friend. He threw a carnation behind the stove and signaled to Marie. When they had left, Marie picked up the carnation and found among the petals a tiny note that told her that money was being raised to bribe her guard, Gilbert. She had no pen or ink so she used a needle to prick out an answer on a scrap of paper, which she handed to Gilbert. The guard was confused by the offer of a bribe of a substantial amount of money. He waited five days before he filed an official report to his superiors. Marie was placed under heavy guard after that, and on October 16, 1793, was executed.

THE LAST KING KILLED BY A MONKEY
King Alexander of Greece died in 1920, after his pet monkey bit him.

THE LAST KING OF THE SAXONS
King Harold, who was defeated and slain at the Battle of Hastings, 1066.

THE LAST KING OF KANDY
Kandy is the capital of the central province of Sri Lanka (Ceylon), located on the Kandy plateau. The last King of Kandy built a beautiful and scenic artificial lake in 1806. Today the city of Kandy is a mountain resort and market center with a population of 100,000 people.

THE LAST NON-ENGLISH-SPEAKING KING OF ENGLAND
George I, King of England from 1714 to 1727, could neither write nor speak the English language. He was the son of Ernest August, Elector of Hanover, and Sophia, granddaughter of James I of England. The German prince was fifty-four years old when he succeeded Queen Anne as sovereign of England, and made no attempt to learn the language of his kingdom.

Last Queen of England Never to Live There

Queen Berengaria, wife of King Richard the Lion-Hearted, was never in England. She married Richard in Cyprus on May 12, 1191, and died at Le Mans in France about 1230 without ever visiting England. Richard was not around England very much either—less than two years, just long enough to collect money for his crusade.

The Last King of the English

King Stephen reigned in England from 1135 to 1154. He was the last king to be known as King of the English. The idea of kingship in Europe seems to have been the rulership over a nation of people rather than over territory. The idea of territorial sovereignty, that is, rulership over land instead of people, grew up during the feudal system. It was not until the reign of King Henry II (1154 to 1189) that the English king was known as King of England.

The Last Pashas

Pasha was the highest honorary title in official usage in the Ottoman Empire. The title was last bestowed in 1934 in Turkey, and in Egypt in 1953.

The Last Ruler of Ancient Egypt

Cleopatra and her son Ptolemy XV (by Julius Caesar) ruled Egypt from 44 to 30 B.C. When Antony and Cleopatra committed suicide, Ptolemy became the last ruler of ancient Egypt. He was killed in 30 B.C. by Octavian (later Augustus, the first Roman emperor), who reduced the status of Egypt to a province of Rome.

THE LAST KAISER

Wilhelm II was the last Kaiser (Emperor). He ruled Germany during World War I and was forced to abdicate in 1918 as part of the price of the Allied peace terms. He was the son of Emperor Frederick III and a grandson of William I and of Queen Victoria; he was also a collateral descendant of Frederick the Great.

THE LAST OF CHINESE IMPERIAL RULE

Chinese imperial rule came to an end with the Chinese Revolution in 1911. On January 1, 1912, Sun Yat-Sen was elected provisional president of the Chinese Republic. On February 12, the last Emperor of China abdicated, ending 3,000 years of Chinese monarchy.

THE LAST GATHERING OF EUROPEAN ROYALTY

The last gathering of European royalty occurred at the marriage of Princess Elizabeth to Lt. Philip Mountbatten on November 20, 1947. The occasion is significant, as several monarchies would fall in the coming years.

Presidential Lasts

LAST PRESIDENT WHOSE SON ALSO BECAME PRESIDENT
John Adams was the last president of the United States whose son, John Quincy Adams, also became president.

LAST WHIG PRESIDENT
Zachary Taylor was the last president who was neither a Democrat nor a Republican. He was a Whig, and defeated Lewis Cass in 1848.

THE LAST UNOFFICIAL PRESIDENT
David Rice Atchison was born in Frogtown, Kentucky, and was president for one day, March 4, 1849. When James K. Polk left office on Saturday night and his successor, Zachary Taylor, delayed the inaugural ceremonies until Monday for religious

reasons, Atchison, President pro tempore of the Senate, unofficially held the post in the interim.

THE LAST FOREIGN-BORN PRESIDENT

William Henry "Tippecanoe" Harrison, the ninth president, was the last "foreign-born" president. His presidency was the shortest in United States history. He died after just one month in office. He was born February 9, 1773, three years before the United States of America was formed, at Berkeley, Charles City County, Virginia. His father was one of the signers of the Declaration of Independence. The Constitution would later require that the president be a native-born citizen and a resident of the United States for at least fourteen years.

THE LAST PRESIDENTIAL CANDIDATE TO WIN THE POPULAR VOTE AND LOSE

Democrat Samuel J. Tilden was the last presidential candidate to win the popular vote but lose the electoral vote. He lost to Rutherford B. Hayes in 1876 by a single electoral vote.

LAST UNITED STATES PRESIDENT TO WIN THE NOBEL PEACE PRIZE

Theodore Roosevelt, 1906.

THE LAST UNITED STATES PRESIDENT WHO WAS NOT A COLLEGE GRADUATE

Harry S Truman was the last American president who was not a college graduate. He attended the Kansas City School of Law from 1923 to 1925.

LAST PRESIDENT TO OWN A SALOON

Abraham Lincoln owned a saloon in Springfield, Illinois, with his friend William Franklin Berry in the 1830s.

THE LAST PRESIDENT WITH IVORY TEETH

The last president of the United States to have false teeth made out of hippopotamus ivory was George Washington.

"THE LAST PRESIDENT OF THE UNITED STATES"

At his inauguration as president, in 1857, James Buchanan, anticipating the future secession of the southern states, remarked, "I am the last president of the United States." He was wrong.

LAST PRESIDENTIAL CAMPAIGN RUN FROM PRISON

Eugene V. Debs, the Socialist Party candidate, ran his campaign for president from prison in 1920. Jailed for sedition, he received nearly 1 million votes.

THE LAST GLIMPSE OF ABRAHAM LINCOLN'S FACE

The last time Lincoln's face was seen was in 1901 when seventeen honored Springfield, Illinois, citizens were asked to peer inside the coffin of Abraham Lincoln to confirm the identity of the occupant. A plumber cut a small window in the lead coffin just over Lincoln's head. The face, with prominent chin and nose, was as distinctive as ever, even covered in the white chalk applied long before by the undertaker on the funeral trip west back in 1865. The suit of black cloth that Lincoln had worn at his second inauguration and final burial was whitened with mildew. After Lincoln was identified, a hole thirteen feet deep was dug below the main catacomb floor. A four-foot base of cement was laid and an iron cage sunk into it. The coffin was lowered into the cage and cement was poured over it, creating a block eight feet deep. These precautions were taken because of numerous attempts (one almost successful) to kidnap Lincoln's body for ransom.

THE LAST PRESIDENT TO SERVE FOUR TERMS

Franklin Delano Roosevelt was the first and the last president to be elected to a third term (in 1940) and a fourth term (in 1944). George Washington had turned down a request that he run for a third term. In 1947 Congress passed the Twenty-second Amendment to the Constitution, limiting future presidents to two terms. It was ratified by thirty-six states in 1951.

LAST PRESIDENT NOT BORN IN A HOSPITAL

Lyndon B. Johnson, the thirty-sixth president, was the last president not born in a hospital. He was born in a farmhouse near Stonewall, Texas, on August 27, 1908.

GEORGE WASHINGTON'S LAST MALE DESCENDANT

The last living male in George Washington's family tree is Bill Washington of Bradley, Illinois. He is the great-great-great-great grandson of Augustine Washington, who was George's father. Bill descended from one of George's half-brothers, Lawrence. There are thousands of Washington's descendants in the United States, but no one else can trace his ancestry back to Augustine Washington. Bill has two daughters, but no sons. His only sister died a few years ago. He has never thrown a silver dollar across the Potomac River but he does share a couple of his famous ancestor's traits: Bill has George's nose, and he doesn't lie.

Last United States President to Weigh Over 300 Pounds
President William Howard Taft tipped the scales at 332 pounds.

Last United States President Impeached
Andrew Johnson. (Nixon resigned but was not impeached.)

The Last Unelected United States President
Gerald R. Ford was never elected vice president or president. He was confirmed United States vice president by the Senate on the resignation of Spiro Agnew in 1973. He succeeded to the presidency on the resignation of Richard Nixon.

Nixon's Famous Last Words
"I don't think you're going to see a great, great uproar in this country about the Republican committee trying to bug the Democratic headquarters," said Richard Nixon four days after the 1972 Watergate burglary, recorded on tape that was released in May 1993.

Garfield's Last Words
On July 2, 1881, President James A. Garfield was shot in the back by assassin Charles J. Guiteau, a former supporter of the president who became bitter after being turned down for a

diplomatic post. The fatal bullet entered Garfield's body a few inches to the side of his spine, but the physicians of the day could not find it, and Garfield lingered for nearly three months before succumbing. He died on September 19, 1881, of the infection caused by the wound and its treatment. On the day before his death, Garfield asked an assistant, "Do you think my name will have a place in human history?" Taken aback, the assistant tried to cheer Garfield up and told him that he had much great work yet to accomplish. "No, my work is done," said Garfield. He asked for a pen and paper and wrote his own epitaph: *Strangulatus Pro Republica* (tortured for the Republic). Then he said to Chief of Staff David G. Swain, "Swain, stop this pain. Oh, Swain!" These were his last words.

LAST WORDS OF JEFFERSON

In addition to his rheumatism Thomas Jefferson had developed an enlarged prostate. He spent his last months in great pain at Monticello, his Virginia estate. Dr. Robley Dunglison, the attending physician, stated that, on July 2, Jefferson lapsed into a "stupor, with intervals of wakefulness and consciousness." Most of the next day he spent unconscious. About 7 P.M. he woke to speak his last words, "Is it the Fourth?" His doctor replied, "It soon will be." He fell back to sleep. He died on July 4, 1826.

THE LAST WORDS OF GROVER CLEVELAND

Grover Cleveland's last words were "I have tried so hard to do right." He then lapsed into a coma and died the next day, June 24, 1908, at 8:40 P.M.

THE LAST WORDS OF JOHN QUINCY ADAMS

Adams was a United States Senator from Massachusetts subsequently elected president (1825–1829), and elected to the House of Representatives thereafter. He suffered a stroke after casting a very loud "No!" against a proposal to decorate certain generals serving in the Mexican War. He was carried away to the Speaker's room and, realizing the seriousness of the situation, said, "This is the end of the earth," and then added either "but I am composed" or "I am content." He died there in the U.S. Capitol Building, Washington, D.C., at 7:30 P.M. on February 23, 1848.

WARREN HARDING'S LAST WORDS

While on a cross-country trip making public appearances, Warren G. Harding fell ill with pneumonia. He was making a recovery at the Palace Hotel in San Francisco, California, on August 2, 1923. Mrs. Harding tried to cheer him up by reading a favorable review of the president which appeared in *The Saturday Evening Post*, "A Calm View of a Calm Man" by Samuel Blythe. "That's good. Go on; read some more," he said. Those were his last words; he died at 7:30 P.M.

MCKINLEY'S LAST WORDS

William McKinley, the twenty-fifth president, addressed the Pan American Exposition in Buffalo, New York, on September 5, 1901. The next day, he was shot by Leon Czolgosz, a twenty-eight-year-old unemployed mill worker of Polish descent. Two operations were performed to remove the bullets. At first the doctors were optimistic; however, McKinley suffered a relapse when gangrene developed around the bullet holes. His last words came at 4:07 P.M.: "It is God's way. His will, not ours, be done."

RUTHERFORD B. HAYES' LAST WORDS

He died on January 17, 1893, at 11 P.M. in Freemont, Ohio. His last words referred to his late wife: "I know that I am going where Lucy is."

JOHN TYLER'S LAST WORDS

During the first full year of the Civil War, Representative-elect Tyler prepared to take his seat in the Confederate house. He checked into the Exchange Hotel in Richmond, where his wife joined him on the tenth of January after having a nightmare that her husband was ill. Two days after her arrival, Tyler fainted in the hotel dining room, and the attending physician diagnosed his condition as biliousness. The former president told his physician, "Doctor, I am going." "I hope not, sir" was his doctor's reply. "Perhaps it is best," responded Tyler. Those were his last words.

JAMES MADISON'S LAST WORDS

Crippled by rheumatism, Madison was confined to his room for the last six months of his life. He was offered stimulants to keep him alive until July 4th so that he could join two former presidents, Adams and Jefferson, in dying on that historic date, but he refused. Sometime after 6 A.M. on June 28, 1836, he had trouble swallowing his breakfast. When one of his nieces asked him, "What is the matter, Uncle James?" he replied, "Nothing more than a change of mind, my dear," and with that, his head dropped. He died of heart failure.

LAST WORDS OF JOHN ADAMS

John Adams was invited to celebrate the nation's fiftieth birthday party in Boston, but he was too weak to venture outside his home in Quincy, Massachusetts. On the morning of July 4, 1826, he lapsed into a coma in his upstairs bedroom. Shortly after noon he rallied long enough to utter these last words: "Thomas Jefferson still . . ." The final word was indistinct but was thought to be "survives." But Jefferson lay dying in Virginia. In an extraordinary and ironic coincidence, the second and third presidents, who had been so passionately involved in the securing of American independence (and who were fierce political rivals thereafter), both died on the fiftieth anniversary of the Declaration of Independence.

LAST PRESIDENT BORN IN A LOG CABIN

James Garfield, the twentieth president of the United States, was born in 1831 in a log cabin on a frontier farm in Cuyahoga County, Ohio.

THE LAST IN THE LINE OF SUCCESSION TO THE UNITED STATES PRESIDENCY

Article II of the Constitution gives Congress the power to determine the presidential order of succession should both the President and Vice President die or become incapacitated, or be disqualified from office. The law currently in effect, passed in 1947, puts the Speaker of the House first in line, followed by the President pro tempore of the Senate. The order of succession then goes through the members of the Cabinet in the order in which the executive departments were established, beginning with the Secretary of State. The Secretary of Education is thirteenth, or, last, in line.

THE LAST PRESIDENT OF THE CONTINENTAL CONGRESS
Cyrus Griffin of Virginia was elected the last president of the Continental Congress January 22, 1788.

THE LAST SENTENCE OF LINCOLN'S GETTYSBURG ADDRESS
"It is rather for us to be here dedicated to the great task remaining before us: that from these honored dead we take increased devotion to that cause for which they gave the last full measure of devotion, that we here highly resolve that these dead shall not have died in vain, that this nation under God shall have a new birth of freedom, and that the government of the people, by the people, for the people shall not perish from the earth."

LINCOLN'S LAST PLAY
President Abraham Lincoln was watching *Our American Cousin* on Friday, April 14, 1865, at Ford's Theatre in Washington, D.C., when he was assassinated.

THE LAST PRESIDENT TO FIGHT A DUEL
Andrew Jackson fought a duel and killed Charles Dickinson on May 30, 1806, in Kentucky. The duel occurred before Jackson served as president of the United States of America from 1829 to 1837.

Calvin Coolidge Has the Last Word

Despite his reputation as a stern man of few words, Calvin Coolidge had a sharp wit. At a press conference, in an exchange with a reporter, he confirmed that he was going to a fair the next day. The reporter asked: "It isn't likely you'll be saying anything tomorrow at the fair?" The president's last retort of the day: "No. I am going as an exhibit." The reporter turned red and slunk to the back, and the press conference ended.

The Last of President Nixon

The last day of Richard Nixon's presidency was August 9, 1974, when he resigned from office as a result of the Watergate scandal.

Last President Whose Grandfather Was President

In 1889, at age fifty-five, Benjamin Harrison was inaugurated into the office of president of the United States. His grandfather, William Henry Harrison, was also president.

The Last President Not to Use "I" in His Inaugural

Theodore Roosevelt, the twenty-fifth president of the United States, was the last president not to use the word "I" in his inaugural address.

The Last President Elected by Men Only

Woodrow Wilson, the twenty-seventh president of the United States, was the last president to be elected only by men. In 1920, the Nineteenth Amendment to the Constitution of the

United States extended the vote to women. The first president women helped to elect was Warren G. Harding.

THE LAST PRESIDENT TO CULTIVATE MARIJUANA

Thomas Jefferson, the third president of the United States of America, an advocate of an agrarian democracy, grew *Cannabis sativa* (marijuana) on his plantation. George Washington also grew pot on his plantations. Jefferson was the last, as far as we know.

THE LAST COLONY IN AFRICA FOUNDED BY FORMER SLAVES

Liberia, on the west coast of Africa, was founded by the American Colonization Society as a home for free blacks. Its capital was named Monrovia in honor of President James Monroe.

THE LAST FREEDOM

President Franklin D. Roosevelt made a speech to Congress on January 6, 1941, in which he spoke of the Four Freedoms: the first was freedom of speech and expression; the second, freedom of religion; the third, freedom from want. The fourth and last freedom was freedom from fear.

Civil War Lasts

THE LAST STATE TO JOIN THE CONFEDERACY

Tennessee was the last state to join the Confederate States of America. It voted to secede from the United States of America on June 8, 1861.

LAST DAY OF THE CIVIL WAR

Kirby Smith surrendered all Confederate troops west of the Mississippi River on May 26, 1865.

STONEWALL JACKSON'S LAST COMMAND

Confederate General Thomas (Stonewall) Jackson's famous last words, after suffering a fatal wound inflicted by his own troops during the Battle of Chancellorsville: "Let us cross over the river and rest under the shade of the trees."

ROBERT E. LEE'S LAST ADDRESS TO HIS TROOPS

The Confederate general gave his last address to his troops, general order no. 9, on April 10, 1865, at Appomattox, Virginia, one day after formally surrendering to Ulysses S. Grant. "After four years of arduous service, marked by unsurpassed courage and fortitude, the Army of Northern Virginia has been compelled to yield to overwhelming numbers and resources. I need not tell the survivors of so many hard-fought battles, who have remained steadfast to the last, that I have consented to this result from no distrust of them: but feeling that valor and devotion could accomplish nothing that could compensate for the loss that would have attended the continuation of the contest. I have determined to avoid the useless sacrifice of those whose past services have endeared them to their countrymen. By the terms of agreement, officers and men can return to their homes and remain there until exchanged. You will take with you the satisfaction that proceeds from the consciousness of duty faithfully performed; and earnestly pray that a merciful God will extend to you his blessing and protection. With an unceasing admiration of your constancy and devotion to your country, and a grateful remembrance of your kind and generous consideration of myself, I bid you an affectionate farewell." On the next day General Lee took formal leave of his army.

THE LAST SURVIVING NEGRO VETERAN OF THE CIVIL WAR

Joseph Clovese, the last surviving Negro veteran of the Civil War, died July 13, 1951. He was born circa 1844. He deserted his plantation master and joined the Union Army as a drummer boy. He later enlisted in a Negro unit.

LAST CIVIL WAR VETERAN

The last American Civil War veteran was Walter Williams (November 14, 1842–December 19, 1959), who died at the age of

117. President Eisenhower ordered flags flown at half mast to honor Civil War veterans. However, investigators failed to find Williams's Confederate service record and suggested that he was only five years old when the war broke out. If this is true, then William A. Lundy, who died in September 1957, was the last surviving Civil War veteran.

LAST SOLDIER TO DIE IN CIVIL WAR FIGHTING

Private John J. Williams, a Union soldier of the 34th Indiana, was shot on May 13, 1865, at the battle of Palmetto Ranch, Texas.

THE LAST CIVIL WAR GENERAL

The last surviving Civil War general was the lieutenant general of the Confederate armies, Simon Bolivar Buckner, who lived until 1914. His son and namesake was a United States general during World War II and was killed on the battlefield.

LAST SHOT OF THE CIVIL WAR

The last shot of the Civil War was a blank. It was fired eleven weeks and three days after Appomattox. The scene took place in the ice-encrusted Bering Strait at the entrance to the Arctic Ocean. A strange black-hulled steamer, heavily armed, came upon a fleet of Yankee whalers on June 28, 1865. The big craft flew an American flag, but soon fired a warning blank, doffed her colors, and ran up the symbol of her trade, the Confederate flag.

LAST CASUALTIES OF THE CIVIL WAR

The last soldiers killed in the Civil War were three Confederate soldiers who refused to accept Lee's surrender. On May 22, 1865, a Virginian named Bordunix and two comrades set out to attack 500 Federal troops at the courthouse in Floyd, Virginia. The Federals were taken by surprise, and when the three Confederates fired on them, two Union soldiers fell wounded. The Federals gave chase to a graveyard six miles away and wanted to take the three rebels alive, but angry spectators urged the troops to fight to the death. The Federals fired one synchronized round of over 300 shots. The Confederate soldiers were killed and buried where they fell.

LAST CONFEDERATE STATE TO BE READMITTED TO THE UNION

The state of Georgia, July 15, 1870. Each of the eleven Confederate states' legislatures had to approve the Thirteenth, Fourteenth, and Fifteenth Amendments before they were readmitted.

Musical Lasts

BEETHOVEN'S LAST SYMPHONY

Beethoven's last symphony was his Ninth, whose fourth movement includes the chorale based on Schiller's "Ode to Joy" and is now known as the United Nations theme.

GUSTAV MAHLER'S LAST SYMPHONY

Mahler was known as an extremely superstitious man, and so he wrote only nine symphonies because his role model, Beethoven, had written just nine before his death. For years, Mahler postponed starting a tenth symphony because of his superstition. Finally, in 1911, he began work on his tenth and last symphony, which remains unfinished because he died that year.

THE LAST BEETHOVEN HEARD OF HIS OWN MUSIC

When he began work on his Third Symphony, Beethoven planned to dedicate it to Napoleon. However, as he was working on the score in Vienna, Beethoven was forced to take shelter from the shelling of the city by the artillery of Napoleon's invading army. The noise had a severe impact on Beethoven's hearing, which was already in decline. The Third Symphony was probably the last Beethoven heard of his own music. In anger, Beethoven renamed the work the *Eroica* and added the second movement's funeral march, which is today played upon the death of great leaders.

THE LAST OF THE CYLINDER RECORDS

Cylinder records were last sold in 1915, and were replaced by 78 RPM flat records.

GILBERT AND SULLIVAN'S LAST OPERETTA

William Schwenck Gilbert and Arthur Seymour Sullivan opened their last operetta, *The Grand Duke*, on March 7, 1896.

THE BEATLES' LAST RECORDING SESSION

Working on the roof of Apple Studios in London, the Beatles recorded "Get Back" on January 30, 1969.

THE LAST BACH COMPOSITION

The last composition of Johann Sebastian Bach (1685–1770), *Die kunst der Fuge*, was unfinished at his death.

Enrico Caruso's Last Performance

The Italian tenor, regarded as the greatest opera singer of the twentieth century, gave his last performance on Christmas Eve, 1920, in New York. He had suffered a throat hemorrhage earlier that month while performing at the Brooklyn Academy of Music, but was able to sing one last time at the Metropolitan Opera. He died the next year.

The Last 78 RPM Records

In Great Britain EMI withdrew its last 78 RPM records from their catalog on March 31, 1962. An exception to the last of the 78s was the release of a limited edition by EMI in 1992 of "Hear My Song" by Irish tenor Josef Locke. In the United States 78s ceased to be produced by 1957—with a few exceptions.

The Last Stradivarius

The world's finest violin maker was arguably Italian Antonius Stradivarius of Cremona. His finest instruments were made after 1700 and his last extant label is dated 1737, the year of his death.

The Last of Janis Joplin

Janis Joplin died of an accidental overdose of heroin at the Landmark Hotel in Los Angeles on October 4, 1970. Her body was cremated, and her ashes were scattered from an airplane along the coastline of southern California.

Jimi Hendrix's Last Concert

Jimi Hendrix's last concert was on the Isle of Wight off the English coast in August of 1970. He performed with Billy Box and Original Experience member Mitch Mitchell on drums. He spent the night of September 18, 1970, at his girl friend Monika Danneman's West London flat. Leaving the message "I need help bad, man" on his manager Charles Chandler's answering machine, he died about 10:20 A.M.. He was twenty-seven. The coroner was unable to find persuasive evidence of either accidental death or suicide and reported an open verdict. In December 1993, Scotland Yard reopened the investigation of his death.

LAST LINE OF "THE FARMER IN THE DELL"

"The cheese stands alone."

Disaster Lasts

THE LAST VOYAGE OF THE *TITANIC*

It was also the maiden voyage for the British liner. She crashed into an iceberg in the North Atlantic, south of Newfoundland, and sank on April 14–15, 1912. More than 1,500 lives were lost. The *Titanic* was touted as the fastest ship afloat and unsinkable.

THE LAST MESSAGE FROM THE *TITANIC*

The last message washed ashore on a beach near Bonavista, Newfoundland, Canada, in 1993. The message, written on faded pink stationery, and stuffed in a champagne bottle, read: "The unsinkable *Titanic* is going down, and we are going down with her. Please pray for us. May God rest our souls."

BELOW THE LAST LINE OF THE THERMOMETER

On February 2, 1947, the town of Snag in the Yukon reported the lowest recorded temperature in North America when the mercury dropped below the last line on the thermometer, at minus 80 degrees. The temperature was officially recorded as minus 81 degress Fahrenheit, and an unofficial guess places the low at minus 83 degrees.

LAST DAYS OF POMPEII

The last days of Pompeii came when Mount Vesuvius, located near Naples, Italy, erupted on August 24–26, 79 A.D. The 4,190-foot Vesuvius scattered clouds of hot mud, stones, and ashes throughout the region of Naples Bay. Three towns in the area—Pompeii, Herculaneum, and Stabiae—were covered in the volcanic ash, and about 10 percent of the region's population was killed. Pompeii and Herculaneum were completely buried.

THE *LUSITANIA'S* LAST VOYAGE

The Cunard liner, returning from a trip to New York, was torpedoed and sunk by a German submarine off Old Head of Kinsal, Ireland, on May 7, 1915, and 1,198 lives were lost.

In 1916, a British seaman saw a bottle bobbing in the North Atlantic. He fished it from the water, opened it, and read the last message from the *Lusitania* before it sank: "Still on the deck with a few people. The last boats have left. We are sinking fast. The orchestra is still playing bravely. Some men near me are praying with a priest. The end is near. Maybe this note will . . ." And there it ended.

THE LAST TIME PEOPLE WERE KILLED BY A GIANT WAVE OF MOLASSES

The skyline in the North End section of Boston, Massachusetts, was dominated by a 90-foot treacle (molasses) storage tank on Copp's Hill Terrace off Salem Street. One day in 1919 it exploded, and 13,500 tons of treacle spewed onto the community. A wave of treacle crested 50 feet high and moved at 35 miles per hour, swallowing eight buildings, engulfing over 100 people, and leaving twenty-one people dead. The area smelled like molasses for years.

WOMEN AND CHILDREN LAST

These are three instances of disasters at sea where women and children came last:

1. The *Phoenix* (Lake Michigan, 1847). A fire in the boiler room swept the length of the liner and the crew crowded into the only two available lifeboats. Passengers, including women and children, jumped overboard and attempted to hang onto the sides of the boats, but were pushed away. Estimated dead: 190–250.

2. The *Arctic* (off the south coast of Newfoundland, 1854). The *Arctic* began to sink after a collision with another vessel. The entire crew ignored the captain's orders and made for the lifeboats, leaving the captain, women, and children. Of 435 aboard, only sixty-one crewmen and twenty-four passengers—all male—survived.

3. The *Morning Star* (Lake Erie, 1868). The *Morning Star* rammed into the *Courtlandt*, a cargo ship. Both boats sank as one. Only after the all-male crew had secured places in the two lifeboats were a few of the *Morning Star*'s first-class passengers (among them women and children) allowed to clamber aboard.

THE LAST OF KRAKATOA

On August 27, 1883, the volcanic island of Krakatoa in Indonesia's Sunda Strait blew up in what is one of the largest explosions in recorded history. Tidal waves resulting from the cataclysmic eruption claimed more than 36,000 lives in Java and Sumatra.

Science Lasts

TELOSPHOBIA

The fear of being last.

THE LAST ELEMENT

The last element discovered (so far) was Element 109, left unnamed, in 1982 by West German scientists.

THE LAST WONDER OF THE WORLD

The pyramids of Egypt are the oldest and the last survivors of the seven wonders of the ancient world.

THE LAST PLANET

Pluto was the last planet discovered in our solar system, located in 1930 by Clyde Tombaugh. He found it precisely where Percival Lowell of the Lowell Observatory had predicted it would be. Pluto's mean distance from the sun is 3.666 billion miles (5.9 billion kilometers). The name Pluto was chosen because it incorporates Lowell's initials.

LAST PLANET IN LINE FROM THE SUN

Since the late 1980s, Neptune has held this distinction. Although Pluto is officially the most remote planet from the sun, its orbit is so eccentric that, at some times, like now, it actually comes closer to the sun than does Neptune. In fact, Neptune will be the farthest planet from the sun until 1998.

THE LAST CONTINENT

Antarctica was the fifth and last continent to be discovered. On February 7, 1821, John Davis made the first landing at what is now Hughes Bay on the Antarctic Peninsula.

THE LAST TIME THE MEDITERRANEAN SEA WAS DRY

The Mediterranean Sea was dry land until about 2 million years ago, when the Atlantic Ocean broke through at the Straits of Gibraltar. It took 100 years for the sea to fill up.

THE LAST MOON ROCKS

The last supply of moon rocks was ferried back from the moon on December 13, 1972. Apollo 17 brought back 243 pounds of lunar rocks, bringing the total for the six American lunar expeditions to 841.6 pounds.

THE LAST OF RED DYE NO. 2

Red dye No. 2, the most frequently used dye in drugs, food, and cosmetics, was banned by the United States Food and Drug Administration on February 12, 1976, after studies indicated the dye was carcinogenic.

EARTH'S LAST FRONTIER CONQUERED

The deepest (36,198 feet/11,033 meters) known depression on the face of the earth is variously known as Marianas Trench, Marianas Trough, or Marianas Deep. It is on the floor of the Pacific Ocean 210 miles (338 kilometers) southwest of Guam. In 1960 two men in a United States Navy bathyscaphe reached the bottom.

Shakespeare Lasts

JULIET'S LAST NAME

Romeo and Juliet's Juliet was a Capulet. Romeo was a Montague.

SHAKESPEARE'S LAST AGE OF MAN

In *As You Like It* Shakespeare describes the ages of man. The seventh and last is: "Last scene of all,/That ends this strange eventful history,/Is second childishness, and mere oblivion,/Sans teeth, sans eyes, sans taste, sans everything." (Act II, scene 7.)

SHAKESPEARE'S LAST PLAY

His last play, a comedy, may have been *The Two Noble Kinsmen*, published in 1634. But this play is of doubtful authorship and may have been written in collaboration with John

Fletcher. Shakespeare's last uncontested play was the tragi-comedy *The Tempest*, first published in 1623.

THE LAST SYLLABLE

"Tomorrow, and tomorrow, and tomorrow,/Creeps in this petty pace from day to day,/To the last syllable of recorded time;/And all our yesterdays have lighted fools/The way to dusty death. Out, out, brief candle!" (*Macbeth*, Act V, scene 5.)

THE LAST TASTE

"As the last taste of sweets, is sweetest . . ." (*Richard II*, Act II, scene 1.)

The Lasts of Art and Literature

LAST WORDS OF EUGENE O'NEILL
"I knew it. I knew it. Born in a hotel room—and God damn it—died in a hotel room." (November 27, 1953)

THE LAST YEARS OF OSCAR WILDE
Oscar Wilde lived out the last three years of his life in France under the assumed name of Sebastian Melmoth.

MARK TWAIN'S LAST RIVERBOAT
Samuel Langhorne Clemens (1835–1910), who was born in Florida, Missouri, last piloted a boat on the Mississippi River in 1861, when he gave up river work to travel west as a confidential secretary to his brother Orion, newly appointed secretary to the territorial governor of Nevada.

HORACE ON LAST DAYS

(Quintus Horatius Flaccus, 65–68 B.C.) "Think to yourself that every day is your last: the hour to which you do not look forward will come as a welcome surprise." (*Epistles*, Book I, epistle i, iv, 13.)

THE LAST CHAPTER OF *GONE WITH THE WIND*

Margaret Mitchell, author of the Pulitzer Prize–winning book *Gone with the Wind*, reportedly wrote the last chapter first, the first chapter next, and the rest in no particular order. Mitchell never wrote another book. She was struck by an automobile and died from her injuries on August 16, 1949.

THE LAST WORK OF ERNEST HEMINGWAY

The last complete work by this American novelist and short story writer (1899–1961) is *Islands in the Stream*.

THE LAST ROSE OF SUMMER

Thomas Moore wrote:

> 'Tis the last rose of summer,
> Left blooming alone;
> All her lovely companions
> Are faded and gone.

THE LAST BOOK BY JAMES JOYCE

The last book by James Joyce is *Finnegans Wake*.

THE LAST MAN AT THE LAST SUPPER

In Leonardo da Vinci's masterpiece, the last man on the right at the "Last Supper" was Judas Iscariot. He was also the thirteenth and, to compound it for the superstitious, Judas is seen spilling salt.

THE LAST LINE IN *A TALE OF TWO CITIES*

The last line in Charles Dickens's *A Tale of Two Cities* was spoken by Sydney Carton: "It is a far, far better thing that I do, than I have ever done; it is a far, far better rest that I go to than I have ever known."

THE LAST WORDS OF *A CHRISTMAS CAROL*

The last words of *A Christmas Carol*, written in 1843 by Charles Dickens: "And so, as Tiny Tim observed, God Bless us, every one!"

THE LAST NOVEL BY AGATHA CHRISTIE

The last novel published by Agatha Christie was *Murder from the Past*. She wrote it around 1940 but specified in her will that it was to be published after her death. She died January 12, 1976.

VAN GOGH'S LAST LETTER

The Dutch Post-Impressionist painter's last letter was to his brother Theo, dated July 24, 1890. Van Gogh, who suffered from grave mental illness, wrote, "I paint as a means to make life bearable." He shot himself and died in his brother's arms two days later. He was buried at Auvers-sur-Oise, France. His devoted brother, who died six months later, was buried in the same grave.

THE LAST TRAGEDY OF SOPHOCLES

Sophocles was a Greek tragic poet and dramatist, author of *Oedipus Rex*, which Aristotle cited as an example of a perfect tragedy. Sophocles wrote his last tragedy, *Oedipus at Colonus*, in 406 B.C., just before he died. It was produced by his son five years later.

THE LAST WORDS OF CEZANNE'S PARROT

Paul Cezanne, the French painter, had a favorite pet parrot whom he had taught to speak. The parrot's last words were "Cezanne is a great painter!" Those were the only words Cezanne had taught him.

THE LAST LIVING ARTIST TO BE EXHIBITED IN THE LOUVRE

The Louvre, noted for its collection of works by old masters such as Rembrandt, Rubens, Titian, and Leonardo da Vinci, has a rule that states the museum will not exhibit an artist's work until he has been dead for at least sixty years. The last living artist to be exhibited at the Louvre was Georges Braque, for whom the museum made an exception. Braque (1881–1963), a French painter who was influenced by Cezanne and explored form and structure with Picasso, veered away from the hard lines of cubism in his last years and developed a more graceful style in his still life paintings.

THE LAST OF VOLTAIRE'S REMAINS

François Marie Arouet de Voltaire, the great French philosopher, thinker, and writer who lived in the seventeenth and eighteenth centuries, spent much of his life exerting himself against judicial arbitrariness. Because he would not sign a retraction of his writings to satisfy the church, he could not get a Christian burial. He died in Paris at the age of eighty-four in 1778. An abbot friend of his secretly buried him in Champagne, a region in northeast France. His remains were exhumed and brought back to Paris in 1791 and buried in the Pantheon, a mausoleum for illustrious Frenchmen. That was the last time Voltaire's body was seen. In 1864 the tomb was opened and found empty.

THE LAST IDEA FOR A SHERLOCK HOLMES STORY

Shortly before his death in 1930, Sir Arthur Conan Doyle concocted a last idea for a plot for a Sherlock Holmes story involving a murder committed by a man on stilts. Regretfully, the story was found among his unpublished papers, unfinished, and the public was denied of a final Holmes and Watson adventure.

LAST OF CERVANTES

Miguel de Cervantes Saavedra was Spain's foremost writer and the author of what is possibly the world's first novel, *Don Quixote*. Cervantes, still poor and unknown, spent the last year of his life in a rented house at the corner of the Calle de Leon and Calle de Cervantes in Madrid, where he died in 1616. Between 1582 and 1587, Cervantes wrote more than twenty plays, only two of which survive.

SARAH BERNHARDT'S LAST FILM ROLE

Sarah Bernhardt, even into old age, remained the divine Sarah, an actress without peer in her time. Her last home, from 1898 on, was 56 Boulevard Péreire in Paris. In March of 1923, too ill to work in a film studio, she performed her last role at her home, in the silent movie *La Voyante*. She finished it only four days before she died. Her house was demolished in 1963. The Théâtre Sarah Bernhardt, where she performed exclusively in Paris for the last twenty-three years of her life, survives at Place du Châtelet. During World War II the Nazi occupiers of Paris changed the name of the theater back to its original name, Théâtre des Nations, after learning that Bernhardt was half Jewish. After the war the theater again took on Sarah's name. Today it is known as Théâtre de la Ville.

THE LAST OF MORIARTY

Professor James Moriarty, Sherlock Holmes's villainous rival, was killed when, locked in combat with Holmes at the edge of Reichenbach Falls in Switzerland, he lost his balance and fell. Holmes, of course, survived.

THE LAST PERRY MASON BOOK

Erle Stanley Gardner wrote seventy-five *Case of the . . .* mysteries starring the fictional lawyer Perry Mason. The first was *The Case of the Velvet Claws* in 1933 and the last was *The Case of the Troubled Trustee* in 1956.

THE LAST OF THE MOHICANS

Uncas, son of Chingachgook, was the last of the Mohicans in James Fenimore Cooper's novel by that name. *The Last of the Mohicans* was published in 1826.

THE LAST WORDS OF GOETHE

Johann Wolfgang von Goethe (1749–1832) was a German poet, dramatist, novelist, and scientist, a genius who embraced most fields of human endeavor. In 1831, the year before he died, he finished the last line of his *Faust*. On his deathbed, the last words he uttered were "More light."

THE LAST LINES (STAGE VERSIONS)

Pippin: "Trapped . . . but happy . . . which isn't too bad for the end of a musical comedy. Ta da!"

Mister Roberts: "Captain, this is Ensign Pulver. I just threw your palm trees overboard. Now what's all this crap about no movie tonight?"

Grease: "Yeah, I'm all choked up."

My Fair Lady: "Eliza? Where the devil are my slippers?"

Camelot: "Run, boy!"

THE LAST VOYAGE OF SINBAD THE SAILOR

A wealthy merchant from Baghdad, Sinbad tells of his adventures in the tenth-century tale *The Arabian Nights' Entertainments*. In his seventh and last voyage he is taken a slave by pirates but escapes.

THE LAST WORDS OF *MARMION*

From *Marmion*, a poem by Sir Walter Scott: "Charge, Chester, charge! On, Stanley, on!"

The Lasts of World War II

DOUGLAS MACARTHUR'S LAST COMMAND
Korea. The five-star general was relieved of duty as commander of allied forces in Korea in April 1951 by President Truman.

SECRETARY OF THE NAVY FRANK KNOX'S FAMOUS LAST WORDS
"No matter what happens, the U.S. Navy is not going to be caught napping," Knox announced on December 5, 1941, just two days before the Japanese attacked Pearl Harbor.

THE LAST AMERICAN SOLDIER EXECUTED BY FIRING SQUAD
Private Eddie Slovik in 1945. He deserted in order to avoid dangerous duty, but was captured, tried by court-martial, and sentenced to death. The execution was personally approved by General Eisenhower. He was shot by his own unit, the 28th In-

fantry Division, in a small town in northeast France, Sainte-Marie-aux-Mines. There were seventy executions by firing squad during World War II, but Slovik's was the only one for desertion. The rest were for rape or murder.

THE LAST ATOM BOMB

At exactly 11:01:58 Japanese time, a plutonium-based weapon, called "Fat Man," exploded over Nagasaki. The city, the most westernized city in Japan at the time (Nagasaki was founded by Portuguese fishermen in 1571) was the target of a B-29 named *Bock's Car*, piloted by Major Charles Sweeney. The bomb exploded 300 yards northeast of a stadium that had been used as the target, between the Mitsubishi Steel & Arms Factory and the Mitsubishi Torpedo Works. The bomb killed nearly 75,000 people instantly. It was the second and last atomic bomb deployed in WWII, and prompted the surrender of Japan to the Allied Forces.

ADOLF HITLER'S LAST HOUR

Hitler committed suicide in a bunker below the Reich Chancellery in Berlin on April 30, 1945.

THE LAST MAJOR WARSHIP SUNK DURING WORLD WAR II

The heavy cruiser *Indianapolis*, traveling without escort after a secret mission to deliver the components of the first atomic bomb to Tinian, an island in the West Pacific, was torpedoed and sunk by a Japanese submarine I-58 at 8:24 A.M. on July 29, 1945. Several hundred sailors survived the torpedo, only to be ravaged by sharks in the greatest shark attack upon humans in history. Rescue efforts were hampered by the secrecy under which the *Indianapolis* had sailed.

LAST RESTING PLACE OF BENITO MUSSOLINI

Benito Mussolini, dictator and warlord in Italy (called "il Duce"), cast his lot with Hitler in 1938 but became thoroughly demoralized and convinced of the eventual defeat of the Axis. He nevertheless established his so-called Salo Republic at Hitler's request in October 1943. From that time until his capture he lived with his mistress Clara Petacci. Their last lodging was in a farmhouse in the village of Bonzanigo. On April 29, 1945, they were captured by communist partisans, taken to the village of Giulino di Mezzegra near Dongo and shot in front of a stone wall. Their bodies were taken to Milan and hung upside down from the girders of a gasoline station in the Piazza Loreto. On August 31, 1957, Benito Mussolini's body was buried at his family tomb. The corpse had been hidden in a rural monastery since 1945.

THE LAST U.S. SECRETARY OF WAR

The last Secretary of War was Kenneth C. Royall in 1947 under President Harry Truman. In that year the Department of War became the Department of Defense.

HITLER'S LAST RECORDED WORDS

Hitler's "Political Testament," as he called it, was brief: "The efforts and sacrifices of the German people in this war have been so great that I cannot believe that they have been in vain.

The aim must still be to win territory in the East for the German people." The last sentence was straight out of *Mein Kampf*. A colonel, entrusted with the message, destroyed it when he learned of Hitler's death while he was still making his way toward the Allies' Western armies. He later reconstructed it from memory.

THE LAST ENTRY IN ANNE FRANK'S DIARY

The last entry in Anne Frank's diary was made Tuesday, August 1, 1944. "I cannot keep this up: I'm watched that closely, I first becme snappish, then sad and finally I turn my heart again. I turn the bad side out, the good side in. I constantly search for the means to become as I want to be so much and what I could be, if . . . there would not live any other people in this world. Your Anne." Here Anne Frank's diary ends. On August 4, 1944, the Grune Polizei invaded the *Achterhuis* where Anne and her family were hiding. All persons were arrested and transported to Dutch and German concentration camps. In March of 1945, two months before the Netherlands were liberated, Anne Frank died in Bergen–Belsen. Only Anne's father returned.

HITLER'S LAST DECISIONS

With the Russians nearing the Potsdamerplatz and getting ready to storm the Chancellery, Hitler was forced, on April 28, 1945, to make the last decisions of his life. By dawn he had married Eva Braun, drawn up his last will and testament, dispatched General Ritter von Greim and Hanna Reitsch, the crack woman test pilot, to rally the Luftwaffe for an all-out bombing of the Russian forces approaching the Chancellery, and ordered them to arrest Himmler as a traitor.

THE LAST SURRENDER

Lee Kuang-Huei, a native of Taiwan who had signed up for military service with Japan during World War II, lived on a remote island in Indonesia for thirty years, thinking the war was still going on. In 1975 some natives accompanied by a local police official found him in his handmade hut. Kuang-Huei flung himself at their feet and asked to be executed as he had offended the emperor by his capture.

LAST DAYS OF WORLD WAR II

The last fighting of World War II in the European theater officially stopped at 11:01 P.M., May 8, 1945. Germany unconditionally surrendered at Rheims on May 7, and the document was ratified at Berlin on May 8.

NEVILLE CHAMBERLAIN'S FAMOUS LAST WORDS

Upon his return to England after his attempted appeasement of Adolf Hitler by removing British objection to Germany's annexation of Czechoslovakia on September 30, 1938, the then Prime Minister uttered these famous last words: "We have peace in our time." Less than a year later, Hitler invaded Poland, and World War II began.

THE LOST SQUADRON LAST SEEN

At 2 P.M. on December 5, 1945, fourteen crewmen aboard five U.S. Navy Avenger bombers took off from their base at Fort

Lauderdale, Florida. They were to fly due east for 160 miles, then north for 40 miles, and return to their base. The five planes and crew were never seen again. On May 16, 1991, American treasure hunters seeking a Spanish galleon made an astonishing discovery. The explorers, diving from the San Francisco research vessel *Deep See*, reported what may be the remains of the lost squadron. The sophisticated craft found five planes in 750 feet of water within two miles of one another, only ten miles off the Florida coast.

THE LAST FÜHRER

Karl Doenitz, Hitler's appointed successor, became Führer upon Hitler's death. He was not a Nazi zealot. Doenitz negotiated the surrender of Germany and was later sentenced to nine years in Spandau prison for war crimes. Upon his release he lived in the town of Aumuhle, West Germany, and died of a heart attack at the age of eighty-nine on December 24, 1980.

THE LAST BATTLE OF WORLD WAR II

The last major battle of World War II began on August 13, 1945, four days after the atomic bombing of Nagasaki, and ended on August 20, 1945, five days after the Japanese offer to surrender the war. The battle took place in central Manchuria, when the Soviet Sixth Guards Tank Army under Marshal R. Y. Malinowsky attacked 750,000 men of the Japanese Kwantung Army. The Soviets, who were mechanized, routed the more numerous Japanese, who were not.

Baseball Lasts

TED WILLIAMS' LAST HOME RUN

Williams, who played for the Boston Red Sox, hit his 531st
and last home run on his last time at bat, in the eighth inning
of a game at Boston's Fenway Park in September 1960.

THE LAST BASEBALL PLAYER TO HIT .400

Ted Williams was the last Major League player to hit over .400.
He hit .406 in 1941 while playing for the Boston Red Sox.

LAST ROOKIE TO BAT OVER .400

Shoeless Joe Jackson was the last rookie to bat over .400 during his official rookie season. He hit .408 for the Cleveland Indians in 1911.

THE LAST WORLD SERIES PERFECT GAME

Don Larsen pitched the last perfect game in the World Series. Pitching for the New York Yankees against the Brooklyn Dodgers in the 1956 World Series, his last out was a strikeout of Dale Mitchell.

LAST BROOKLYN DODGERS GAME AT EBBETS FIELD

Although only 6,702 fans were watching the Brooklyn Dodgers play their last game at Ebbets Field, they went out in style by beating the Pittsburgh Pirates 2–0 on September 26, 1957. They moved from Brooklyn, New York, to California and become the Los Angeles Dodgers. Ebbets Field was demolished in 1960.

THE LAST AMERICAN LEAGUE PITCHER TO GET A BASE HIT IN REGULAR SEASON PLAY

Ferguson Jenkins on October 2, 1974. The following season, the designated hitter rule was introduced.

THE LAST TIME MICKEY MANTLE WORE NUMBER 6

Mickey Mantle wore the number 6 during his rookie season. The rest of his career he wore number 7.

THE LAST TIME A TEENAGE GIRL STRUCK OUT BABE RUTH AND LOU GEHRIG

Virnie Bertrice "Jackie" Mitchell, a seventeen-year-old girl fastball pitcher from Fall River, Massachusetts, was the last and only girl pitcher to strike out Ruth and Gehrig. It happened in Tennessee in 1931. The New York Yankees were to play an exhibition game against the Chattanooga Lookouts, who were owned by Joe Engel. Engel signed Jackie up to pitch and to fill his stadium. The stadium was packed when Jackie took the mound in the middle of the first inning and Ruth came to bat. She threw five pitches and struck him out on a called strike three. Gehrig was up next, and she struck him out with three straight pitches.

The Last Player to Hit in Fifty-six Consecutive Games

Joe DiMaggio, playing for the New York Yankees, got at least one hit in fifty-six consecutive games during the 1941 season.

Roberto Clemente's Last Hit

Roberto Clemente, professional baseball's first Latino superstar, was born in Puerto Rico and for eighteen seasons was right fielder for the Pittsburgh Pirates. He won four National League batting titles, was elected twelve times to the All-Star team, received the National League's Most Valuable Player Award and the World Series' Outstanding Player Award. In his last time at bat in the 1972 season Clemente hit a double to left-center field. That hit was his 3,000th. Only ten other players had 3,000 career hits. Clemente's 3,000th hit also marked his last hit in baseball; he was killed on New Year's Eve, December 31, 1972, while flying relief supplies to earthquake victims in Nicaragua.

Ty Cobb's Last Season

Tyrus Raymond Cobb, known as the Georgia Peach, played his last season for the Philadelphia Athletics in 1928. He joined the Detroit Tigers in 1905 as centerfielder, and in his twenty-four years was one of the most spectacular and brilliant baseball players ever. He had a lifetime batting average of .367. He made 4,191 hits, stole 892 bases, and won twelve batting championships.

Castro's Last Pitch

Fidel Castro, Cuba's Communist dictator, was, by most accounts, a second-string right-handed baseball pitcher for the University of Havana in Cuba in the mid-'40s. A major league scout told him he did not have a major league arm. Castro seized power early in 1959. The last time Castro pitched was just after the revolution, when he played for Los Barbudos (The Bearded Ones) on July 24, 1959. He pitched a scoreless inning, striking out two. It was an exhibition game prior to an International League game between the Sugar Kings and the Rochester Red Wings.

The Last Time Home Plate Was Diamond-Shaped

Home plate was diamond-shaped through 1899. The 1900 baseball season opened with the new pentagon-shaped home plate.

The Last of the Baseball Kranks

In 1883 the term "fan" was coined by St. Louis Browns manager Ted Sullivan when team owner Chris Von der Ahe called the club's followers "fanatics." Sullivan shortened it to "fan." The popular name for a baseball fan until then was "krank."

HANK AARON'S LAST HOME RUN

Henry Louis Aaron, playing for the Atlanta Braves, broke Babe Ruth's long-standing record for career home runs. Batting against Los Angeles Dodger pitcher Al Downing, Hank hit his 715th home run over the the left-field fence of Atlanta Stadium on April 8, 1974. Aaron joined the Milwaukee Brewers in 1975. He hit his 755th and last home run in Milwaukee on July 20th, 1976, playing against the California Angels, with Dick Drago pitching. Aaron knew this was his last home run and wanted to save the ball he had hit, but a kid from the ground crew named Dick Arndt picked up the ball and would not give it to Aaron. The Brewers fired Arndt over it. Years later Aaron offered him $10,000 for it, but he still wouldn't part with it.

JIM THORPE'S LAST TEAM

Jim Thorpe was a Sac and Fox Indian athlete, voted the greatest athlete of the first half of the twentieth century in 1950. The last baseball team that Jim played for was the Boston Braves of the National League.

LAST MIDGET TO BAT

Edward Carl Gaedel, a midget standing 43 inches high, pinch-hit for the St. Louis Browns in a game against the Detroit Tigers. He walked and was replaced by Jim Delsing, the regular outfielder, who ran for him. He never batted again. The plate umpire, Ed Hurley, would not let Gaedel bat until Zack Taylor, the Browns' owner, produced a signed contract with the batter.

JACKIE ROBINSON'S LAST GAME

Brooklyn Dodger and Hall of Famer Jackie Robinson's last Major League game was on the losing end of the seventh game of the World Series against the New York Yankees on October 10, 1956.

LAST NEW YORK GIANTS HOME GAME

On September 29, 1957, the New York Giants played their last baseball game at the Polo Grounds against the Pittsburgh Pirates and lost 9–1.

LOU GEHRIG'S LAST CONSECUTIVE GAME

Lou Gehrig played in 2,130 straight baseball games—every game for almost fourteen full seasons—and set an Iron Man record that still stands today. His 2,130th and last game took place on May 1, 1939. Two years later, he was to die of a neurological disease (amyotrophic lateral sclerosis) that today bears his name, without getting a chance to play another game.

THE LAST TRIPLE-HEADER

On October 2, 1920, the Cincinnati Reds and the Pittsburgh Pirates were the last Major League teams to play a triple-header.

MAJOR LEAGUE BASEBALL'S FAMOUS LAST WORDS

Harry Frazee, the owner of the Boston Red Sox who sold Babe Ruth to the New York Yankees in 1919, said: "Ruth had become simply impossible, and the Boston club could no longer put up with his eccentricities. I think the Yankees are taking a gamble."

LAST LINE OF "CASEY AT THE BAT"

"Mighty Casey has struck out."

BABE RUTH'S ABSOLUTELY VERY LAST TIME AT BAT

During World War II, Johnny Sain of the Boston Braves and Ted Williams were in the service at Chapel Hill, North Carolina, and were taken up to New York to play in an exhibition game before a regular game between the New York Yankees and the Cleveland Indians. Sain was the pitcher for one side and Ruth was managing the other side and put himself in to pinch hit. According to Sain, the umpire wouldn't call a strike, so Ruth walked on four straight pitches. That was his last time at bat.

The Lasts of Sports

PELE'S LAST GAME

Edson Arantes do Nascimento (Pele's real name) was perhaps the greatest player in the history of soccer. He played his last season with the Brazilian national team in 1971. He continued to play with the Santos through the end of the 1974 season.

MANOLETE'S LAST BULLFIGHT

Manuel (Manolete) Rodriguez, Spain's most famous bullfighter, had retired after a thirteen-year career, but his adoring fans brought him back. During his last bullfight, he was gored in the thigh and died from shock and loss of blood on August 28, 1947.

THE LAST YEAR THE NATIONAL HOCKEY LEAGUE
HAD ONLY CANADIAN TEAMS

The last year the National Hockey League was composed entirely of teams representing Canadian cities was 1923. In 1924 Boston became the first American city to be admitted.

LAST TIME THE OLYMPIC MARATHON WAS WON
IN OVER THREE HOURS

In 1904 by Thomas Hicks of the United States in St. Louis, Missouri. It took him three hours, 28.63 minutes. Every race since has been won with a time under three hours.

THE LAST IVY LEAGUE ROSE BOWL WIN

The last Ivy League school to win the Rose Bowl was Columbia in 1933. They defeated Stanford 7–0.

THE LAST TIME PENNSYLVANIA HAD ONLY ONE TEAM
IN THE NATIONAL FOOTBALL LEAGUE

In 1943, during World War II, many players were in the service. There were not enough good football players left to go around, so the Pittsburgh Steelers and the Philadelphia Eagles merged for the 1943 season and played as "The Steagles."

FAMOUS LAST RUN

The Battle of Marathon prompted two Greek runners into extraordinary feats of endurance that have since passed into myth. The first was Pheidippides, the best runner in all of Athens. In 490 B.C. King Darius of Persia sent his army to attack the Athenians on the plain of Marathon. The outnumbered Athenians sent Pheidippides to Sparta to request help. He covered the 140 miles to Sparta in one day and night and ran back to Marathon in the same amount of time. With little time to rest, he joined the battle as an infantryman and helped the Athenians to defeat the powerful Persians. The Athenian commander asked another Greek runner (whose name has not survived, and who is therefore often confused with Pheidippides) to carry the news of victory to Athens, 22 miles and 1,470 yards away. The unfortunate Greek covered the distance in short order and staggered the last yards into the central marketplace of Athens, shouting "*Niké! Niké!*" (Victory! Victory!) Then he fell to the ground and died. The modern marathon commemorates this unknown Greek's famous last run.

THE LAST BARE-KNUCKLE FIGHT

John L. Sullivan fought in the last professional bare-knuckle championship fight in history. In 1889 Sullivan beat Jake Kilrain in seventy-five rounds in a boxing ring at Richburg, Mississippi.

JOE LOUIS'S LAST FIGHT

Joe Louis was an American heavyweight boxer who became the world heavyweight boxing champion in 1937 when he knocked out James J. Braddock in the eighth round in Chicago. He retired in 1949; by then he had defended his title twenty-five times, with twenty-one knockouts. He came out of retirement in 1950 and lost a decision to Ezzard Charles. In 1951 he fought and lost by a knockout to Rocky Marciano. This was his last fight, after which he retired for good.

FISCHER'S LAST CHECKMATE
The last day Bobby Fischer held the world chess title was April 3, 1975. He lost it after refusing a match with U.S.S.R. challenger Anatoly Karpov, who became champion by default.

THE LAST OF THE FIRST ICE RINK
The world's first indoor ice skating rink opened on London's Baker Street in 1842. The rink was made from soda crystals. It was less than ideal and was last used in 1876.

THE LAST OF DISCONTINUED OLYMPIC GAMES
• *Cricket.* Held in Paris in 1900. Great Britain defeated France 262–104.
• *Croquet.* Held in Paris in 1900. Aumoitte of France won at singles one ball, Way Delick of France won at singles two ball, and Johin and Aumoitte of France won the doubles.
• *Women's golf.* Held in Paris in 1900. Margaret Abbott of the United States won with a score of 47.
• *Men's golf.* Held in St. Louis in 1904. George Lyon of Canada beat seventy-five other golfers.
• *Jeu de Paume.* Held in London in 1908. Jeu de Paume, also known as court tennis, was the forerunner of modern-day tennis. Jay Gould of the United States and Neville of Great Britain won.
• *Lacrosse.* Held in London in 1908. Canada defeated Great Britain 14–10.
• *Polo.* Held in Paris in 1900. Foxhunters Hurlingham GRB/USA defeated Club Rugby GRB/USA 3–1.

- *Rugby.* Held in Paris in 1924. The underdog United States team defeated France.
- *Tug of War.* Held in Antwerp in 1920. Great Britain took the gold, Holland the silver, and Belgium the bronze.

THE LAST MEN-ONLY OLYMPIC GAMES

The ancient Olympic Games started in 776 B.C. Women, foreigners, slaves, and "dishonored persons" were forbidden to compete. Since men competed naked, Greek women were forbidden to watch. The modern Olympic games, first held in Athens in 1896, included only men through the London games of 1908—women were included for the first time in 1912.

THE LAST PERSON TO HIT A GOLF BALL OUTSIDE THE EARTH'S ATMOSPHERE

Astronaut Alan Shepard, on February 5, 1971, hit a golf ball while on the moon.

ROCKY MARCIANO'S LAST FIGHT

Rocky Marciano (1924–1969), born in Brockton, Massachusetts, was the last boxer to knock out Joe Louis (and only the second boxer to accomplish this feat). His last fight before he retired in April of 1956 was against Archie Moore in New York City on September 21, 1955. He won by a knockout in the ninth round and retained the world heavyweight championship.

The Lasts of Sea and Space

LAST MEN ON THE MOON

The last two men on the moon were Eugene A. Cernan, mission commander of Apollo 17, and astronaut Harrison H. Schmitt. They left behind a plaque on the moon that reads: "Here man completed his first explorations of the moon. May the spirit of peace in which we came be reflected in the lives of all mankind." They departed the moon at 12:38 (EST) on December 13, 1972. In contrast to the elegant phrases of the plaque he left behind, Cernan's exact words at liftoff were "Okay, let's get this mother out of here."

MAGELLAN'S LAST LEG

The last completed leg of the round-the-world-journey attempted by Ferdinand Magellan was from Guam to Mactan, an island in the Philippines. There he was killed on April 27, 1521, denying him the glory of circumnavigating the globe.

THE LAST OF *CHALLENGER*

The space shuttle *Challenger* came to a tragic end as millions watched on television when it exploded 74 seconds after liftoff at Cape Canaveral, Florida, on January 28, 1986. All seven astronauts died, including Christa McAuliffe, a thirty-seven-year-old teacher from Concord, New Hampshire. She was the first private citizen chosen for the United States space flight program.

SPUTNIK'S LAST DAY

Sputnik landed on October 4, 1958, after three months in orbit. The first-ever satellite had been launched into space by the U.S.S.R.

Lasts Across America

THE LAST RIDE OF THE PONY EXPRESS

The Pony Express service ran between St. Joseph, Missouri, and Sacramento, California. It was first offered April 3, 1860. There were eighty riders and four hundred horses, and they covered 1,966 miles with 190 stops along the way. The trip took ten days, and the rate was five dollars per letter. The Pony Express was put out of business when the Transcontinental Telegraph was made available to the public on October 24, 1861. The Pony Express's final haul reached Sacramento two days later, on October 26, 1861.

THE LAST FACE CARVED ON MOUNT RUSHMORE

The original idea was to honor three western heroes, Jim Bridger, John Colter, and Kit Carson. When the noted sculptor Gutzon Borglum was given the job, he selected Mount Rushmore as the site and suggested that the monument be presidential instead. The four presidents—Washington, Jefferson, Lincoln, and Theodore Roosevelt—were chosen to reflect the first 150 years of American history. It took fourteen years to blast and chisel and almost a million dollars to complete. President Calvin Coolidge officially dedicated Mount Rushmore a national memorial on August 10, 1927. Borglum died in March of 1951 but his son Lincoln continued another seven months before running out of funds. The last face to be worked on, but never completed, was Roosevelt's.

THE LAST TIME BROOKLYN, NEW YORK, WAS ITS OWN CITY

That was in 1897. Brooklyn was incorporated as a village (Brooklyn Ferry) in 1816, and the township of Brooklyn was chartered as a city in 1834. When Williamsburg was absorbed in 1855, Brooklyn became the third-largest city in the United States. In 1898, with a population of 1 million, Brooklyn became a borough of New York City.

CRAZY HORSE'S LAST RESTING PLACE

The great Sioux warrior was murdered in jail at Fort Robinson in Nebraska. Family members buried him in a location that has never been publicly revealed.

THE LAST OF BRIGHAM YOUNG'S CHILDREN

The Mormon leader fathered Fanny, the last of his fifty-seven children by twenty-seven wives, in 1870. She lived until 1950.

THE LAST TIME HARVARD UNIVERSITY WAS CALLED CAMBRIDGE

The University at Cambridge was founded in 1636 and in 1838 renamed for John Harvard, its first benefactor.

THE LAST YEAR THE STATE OF MAINE WAS PART OF MASSACHUSETTS

1819.

THE LAST STATE TO LEGALIZE DIVORCE

On March 17, 1949, South Carolina voters approved legalized divorce, making it the last state to do so.

THE LAST TIME WASHINGTON, D.C., WAS KNOWN AS FEDERAL CITY

George Washington was the last to call the new capital Federal City. He knew of plans to name the new capital of the United States after him but always referred to it as Federal City in typical modesty. Washington, who chose the site for the president's mansion and laid the cornerstone of the Capitol in 1793, never lived in the new city and died before the first building was completed.

THE LAST *H* IN 4-H

The last *H* in the 4-H Club's name stands for "Hand." The other three are "Head, Health, Heart."

THE LAST STATE WHOSE LAND WAS PURCHASED FROM A FOREIGN COUNTRY

Alaska was the last state whose land was purchased from a foreign country: from Russia in 1887 for $7,200,000.

THE LAST TIME AMERICA ONLY HAD MALE BARRISTERS

The last time barristers in America were all male was in the year 1639. In 1640 Margaret Brent, colonial attorney for Cecil Calvert, Lord Proprietor of Maryland, became the first woman attorney in America.

THE LAST OF CAPTAIN KIDD

English-born William Kidd was at one time a wealthy New York landowner who served as a privateer for the Crown against the French. Disease, mutiny, and failure to take prizes apparently caused him to turn pirate. He was tried and hanged in London, May 23, 1701. It is said that in the spring of 1699 he paid a visit to an old friend in Narragansett, Rhode Island, and left behind his fabled treasure for later retrieval.

VASSAR'S LAST ALL-GIRL CLASS

The last time Vassar only permitted women at the college was in the year 1969. The following year it opened its enrollment to men.

BEN FRANKLIN'S LAST PUBLIC ACT

Benjamin Franklin, American printer, author, inventor, and diplomat, was born in Boston, Massachusetts, on January 17, 1706. Franklin lived out the last five years of his life at his daughter's house in Philadelphia, Pennsylvania. His last public act was to sign a memorandum to Congress on February 12, 1790, asking for the abolition of slavery. He died in Philadelphia on April 17, 1790.

LAST CIGARETTE PACKAGES IN AMERICA WITHOUT HEALTH WARNINGS

The last cigarette packages without the warning "Caution: cigarette smoking may be hazardous to your health" rolled off the assembly line in early 1966.

THE LAST WE'LL SEE OF NIAGARA FALLS

Niagara Falls is one of the most majestic and spectacular natural sites in North America. Located on the international boundary line between the cities of Niagara Falls, New York, and Niagara Falls, Ontario, it is an important source of hydroelectric power. Since the time they were formed 10,000 years ago the falls have eroded about ten miles back up the Niagara River; at that rate, the tremendous force of the water will eat through the limestone base and the falls will disappear by the year 23,993 A.D.

LAST POINTS OF LAND IN AMERICA

Last point north: Point Barrow, Alaska. Last point south: South Cape, Hawaii. Last point east: West Quoddy Head, Maine. Last point west: Cape Wrangell, Alaska.

THE LAST MOXIE

The once-famous and popular soft drink (it contributed a word to the English language that indicated spirit and spunk) was last seen on the store shelves around August 27, 1990, when it was abandoned as a product by its bottler.

THE LAST DAY OF ISMAY, MONTANA

In July 1993, the small town of Ismay in Montana voted to change the town's name to "Joe" in honor of the star quarterback. (Actually they used the name "Joe, Montana" just during the football season, reverting back to Ismay right after the Super Bowl.)

THE LAST OF AMERICA'S FIRST MAGAZINES

America's first two magazines were founded within three days of each other in Philadelphia. Benjamin Franklin's *General Magazine, and Historical Chronicle for all the British Plantations in America* appeared and disappeared in the same year, 1741. Andrew Bradford's *American Magazine, A Monthly View of the Political State of the British Colonies* suffered the same fate.

THE LAST DAY OF THE OF FIRST DAILY NEWSPAPER IN AMERICA

The first daily newspaper in the United States appeared on September 21, 1784. The *Pennsylvania Packet and Daily Advertiser* was published in Philadelphia, Pennsylvania, by Daniel C. Claypoole and John Dunlop. It was published for the last time on December 31, 1790.

THE LAST ISSUE OF THE ORIGINAL *SATURDAY EVENING POST*

On February 8, 1969, the last issue of *The Saturday Evening Post* was published. The magazine was first published on August 4, 1821. In the 1970s the magazine was resurrected and is now issued nine times a year.

Lasts Around the World

THE LAST POINT SOUTH IN EUROPE

The southernmost point in Europe is a point in Gibraltar, Spain. It is further south than any point of land in Greece or Italy.

THE LAST TIME THE UNION JACK WAS
THE OFFICIAL FLAG OF CANADA

February 14, 1956. The next day the Maple Leaf design became the official Canadian flag.

THE LAST CANADIAN PROVINCE

Newfoundland became the tenth and last province of the Dominion of Canada on March 31, 1949. In a 1948 referendum, 78,323 Newfoundlanders voted for confederation while 71,334 chose self-government, a difference of less than 5 percent. A

1950 election picked Joey Smallwood as the Province's first premier.

THE LAST OF BRITISH RULE IN INDIA

For 346 years Great Britain ruled the Indian subcontinent as a single country. The Indian people fought for their independence, but Muslims demanded a country separate from the Hindus. London, faced with a civil war, created the Indian Independence Act on August 15, 1947, which partitioned the subcontinent into the predominantly Hindu Dominion of India and the mainly Muslim State of Pakistan. In 1971, East Pakistan revolted from West Pakistan and became the independent state of Bangladesh.

THE LAST DAY THE WORLD WAS FREE OF INCOME TAX

January 6, 1789. The next day Great Britain introduced the world's first income tax.

LAST POINT SOUTH IN AFRICA

The most southern point of land in Africa is located at Cape Agulhas, in South Africa. Most people think it is the Cape of Good Hope (100 miles to the west and north) but Cape Agulhas is actually 29 minutes of latitude further south.

LAST POINT SOUTH IN SOUTH AMERICA

The most southern point in South America is Cape Horn (55 degrees, 59 minutes south latitude).

THE LAST SCOOP OF PHOSPHATE

After nearly ninety years of mining, Nauru, the earth's smallest independent republic, will mine the last scoop of phosphate, a rich fertilizer base, within the next decade. The mining has turned 80 percent of Nauru's landscape into a moonscape, and its 10,000 citizens into one of the highest per capita income people in the world. Prior to 1968 Australia was chief administrator of Nauru, an eight-square-mile island in the South Pacific.

THE LAST POINT NORTH IN EUROPE

The most northern point in Europe is North Cape, a promontory on the island of Magero, off the coast of Norway (70 degrees, 11 minutes north).

THE LAST OF MESOPOTAMIA

In 1922, Iraq was recognized as a kingdom, and known by the ancient Greek name of Mesopotamia no more.

THE LAST OF CONSTANTINOPLE

Now it's Istanbul, not Constantinople. In 1930 the former capital of the Byzantine and the Ottoman Empires changed its name to Istanbul, eight years after Turkey was created out of the Ottoman Empire. However, for many years before that the old part of Constantinople was known as Stamboal.

THE LAST VIKINGS ON GREENLAND

Erik the Red, a criminal banished from his native Norway, came upon and named Greenland around 982 A.D. Two hundred years later the climate grew colder, making living conditions extremely difficult. By the end of the 1300s the last of the Greenland population was wiped out by the bubonic plague.

THE LAST TIME DUBLIN WAS DANISH

The last time Dublin, Ireland, was Danish was 1170, just before Richard Strongbow, second earl of Pembroke, captured the city for the English. In 1172 Henry II and England came to Dublin and granted the city to the "men of Bristole"; it became the seat of English government and center of the Pale.

STANLEY'S LAST AFRICAN EXPEDITION

Welsh-born Henry M. Stanley was the soldier, adventurer, and journalist who found Dr. Livingstone in the African wild. In 1887–89 Stanley made his last expedition in Africa to rescue Emin Pasha, the German governor of the Egyptian Sudan. Having overcome the threats of the Islamic armies of the Mahdi, Stanley's ragtag party finally reached the Pasha only to be told that he did not need or want to be rescued.

HANNIBAL'S LAST ELEPHANT TRIP

The last recorded use of elephants by Hannibal to carry troops and supplies through the Alps was in 218 B.C. This was one of the remarkable military feats in history, employed to wipe out the Roman forces in the Po Valley.

LAST CORNMILL IN NORTHERN IRELAND

The last traditional working cornmill in Northern Ireland is in Crossgar, County Down.

THE LAST CORNMILL IN THE REPUBLIC OF IRELAND

The last traditional working cornmill in Ireland is in Killkenny County.

LAST DAY A WALL DIVIDED BERLIN

The twenty-six-mile Berlin Wall last stood intact on October 3, 1990. The next day the wall was opened, reuniting East and West Germany after forty-five years of separation.

THE LAST TIME ATHENS WAS A SMALL TOWN

Athens, Greece, had a population of 2,000 inhabitants in 1829. By the time the Greek War of Independence of 1821 overthrew the Ottoman Turks who had ruled for 365 years and established modern Greece, Athens had been reduced to a mere village. It has since experienced a resurgence.

LAST DAY OF PRIME MINISTER THATCHER

Margaret Thatcher gave her last speech before the House of Commons on her last day as Prime Minister of Great Britain, November 22, 1990. After eleven years the Parliament gave her a vote of no confidence, due to her introduction of the poll tax.

THE LAST STONE LAID IN BUCKINGHAM PLACE

The last stone of Buckingham Palace, the British Royal residence in London, was laid in 1911. The Palace was designed by architects Webb and Brock.

THE LAST OXFORD COLLEGE FOR MEN ONLY

The last Oxford University college to exclude women students was Oriel College, which did so until September 1985.

MARCOS' LAST RESTING PLACE

Almost four years after his death on September 28, 1989, in Honolulu, Hawaii, the body of former Philippines President Ferdinand Marcos was brought to its last resting place. Corazon Aquino, who had succeeded him as president, had refused to allow the body to be returned. It was stored in an air-conditioned crypt until current president Fidel Ramos made the decision to let the body return to his homeland. Marcos' body was taken, on September 10, 1993, to his hometown of Batac.

ATTILA THE HUN'S LAST DAY

Attila, king of the Huns, was called the Scourge of God. He conquered the eastern Roman empire and the Balkans, and got as far as northern Italy. In 453 A.D. while in Hungary, he died of a hemorrhage while celebrating his wedding.

THE LAST TIME GANDHI WAS JAILED BY THE BRITISH

In 1930, in protest against the British government's salt tax, Mohandas Gandhi led the famous 200-mile march to extract salt from the sea. For this he was imprisoned, but released. In 1942 the British jailed seventy-two-year-old Gandhi for the last time for nationalist activity against the British colonial government.

THE LAST BRICKS IN HADRIAN'S WALL

Hadrian's Wall was an ancient Roman fortification begun in 122 A.D. and completed in 126 A.D. Built on orders of Emperor Hadrian, the wall was 73.5 miles (118.3 kilometers) long and ran across the narrow part of Great Britain from Wallsend on the Tyne River to Bowness at the head of Solway Firth, serving as the northern boundary and defense line of Roman Britain. Sections of the wall (6 feet [1.8 m] high and 8 feet [2.4 m] thick) and many of the blockhouses that were set every Roman mile along it remain.

THE LAST CAMBRIDGE UNIVERSITY COLLEGE TO ADMIT WOMEN

Magdalene College was the last Cambridge University college to admit women students. When they were finally admitted in October 1988, the undergraduate men wore black armbands and carried a coffin throughout the campus.

THE LAST OF WIGS AS THE HEIGHT OF FASHION

In Egypt wigs were worn to protect the head from the sun. The wig became popular in Europe in the seventeenth century. First worn during the reign of Louis XIII of France, who himself wore a wig, the wig became popular in England during the reign of Charles II, when wigs were variously powdered white, scented, and made of plaster of Paris in pink, gray, and blue. By 1788 men began to wear their own hair tied at the back, sometimes powdered. After 1800 long hair for men lost favor, but wigs continued their hold on the professional classes and can be seen today in the official dress of English courts.

THE LAST WESTERN COUNTRY TO GRANT WOMEN THE RIGHT TO VOTE

Switzerland, in 1971.

THE LAST ROSENKOWITZ SEXTUPLET

The last Rosenkowitz sextuplet baby, born January 11, 1974, in Cape Town, South Africa, was Elizabeth. The other five were, in order of birth: Davis, Nicolette, Jason, Emma, Grant.

THE LAST DIONNE QUINT

Marie was the last born. The other four, all sisters, were Annette, Emelie, Yvonne, and Cecile, born May 28, 1934, in Callender, Ontario.

THE LAST OF SIAM

On May 11, 1949, Siam officially became Thailand, which means Land of the Free.

Lasts in U.S. History

THE LAST TIME A DEAD MAN WAS ELECTED GOVERNOR

Under the statutes of the state of Georgia, members of the legislature select a governor if no candidate receives a majority of votes. Governor-Elect Eugene Talmadge died on December 1, 1946, just before the legislature went through the normally perfunctory rite of "publishing the returns and verifying the election." With the governor's chair vacant, legislators proceeded to name Herman Talmadge, son of the dead man, to the state's highest office. But the case was taken to the state Supreme Court. After pondering the testimony presented to them, judges ruled that though Eugene Talmadge was dead when the votes were counted, he had received a majority and had been properly elected governor.

LAST SURVIVOR OF THE PAWTUXET INDIAN NATION

Squanto was the last survivor of the Pawtuxet Indian nation. Legend credits Squanto with teaching the *Mayflower* colonists how to catch fish and dry herring, tap maple trees for their sugar and plant the native corn. Squanto was captured by an English slave trader in 1614, then sold to a Spanish master. He escaped to England and in 1618 returned to his homeland to find all the members of his tribe had been wiped out by a smallpox epidemic.

THE LAST PART OF "REMEMBER THE *MAINE*"

Everybody remembers from their history lessons that an American ship was blown up in Cuba, and the war cry was "Remember the *Maine*." On January 25, 1889, the U.S.S. *Maine* arrived in Havana harbor to protect American interests. While anchored in the middle of Havana harbor, the battleship exploded February 15, 1889, killing 260 members of the crew. The American newspaper headlines blazed: "Remember the *Maine!*" coupled with the last part of the war cry, "To hell with Spain!" That act led to war with Spain over Cuba. By August 9, 1898, when the Spanish–American War was over and peace was signed with Spain, 5,462 Americans had died.

WYATT EARP'S LAST VOTE

Wyatt Earp was the deputy sheriff of Tombstone, Arizona, deputy marshal in Dodge City, Kansas, an outlaw, and one of the American west's enduring legends. He eventually settled in Los Angeles, where he lived out his last days in a small tourist rental court. On Election Day, November 1928, Wyatt got out of his sickbed, and although he was a lifelong Republican and

Protestant, he cast his last vote for Al Smith, a Democrat and Catholic, and for the repeal of Prohibition. At 8:05 Sunday morning on January 13, 1929, Wyatt Earp died at the age of eighty.

THE LAST OF THE FIRST PERMANENT ENGLISH SETTLEMENT IN AMERICA

On May 14, 1607, the London Company established Jamestown, which became the first permanent English settlement in America. The village was built on a marshy peninsula, in what is now an island in southeast Virginia. Disease, starvation, and Indian attacks wiped out most of the colony. The London Company continually sent more supplies and men but after a severe winter in 1609, the remaining population was preparing to return to England. Lord De la Warr arrived with supplies just in time to force them to stay. Jamestown became the capital of Virginia.

The colonists grew tobacco and flourished for a while, but the village was almost completely destroyed during Bacon's Rebellion (1675–1676). When the capital of Virginia was moved to Williamsburg in 1698, it fell into further decay and never recovered. Today the last of Jamestown is the property of the United States government and it is included in the Colonial National Historical Park, except for the land owned by the Association for Preservation of Virginia Antiquities.

THE LAST OF CIGARETTE ADVERTISING ON TELEVISION IN THE UNITED STATES

On December 31, 1970, the last cigarette ad, a commercial for Virginia Slims, ran on the *Tonight Show*. President Richard

Nixon had signed a bill passed by Congress, banning cigarette advertising on radio and television, to go into effect on January 1, 1971.

LAST WORDS IN THE "I HAVE A DREAM" SPEECH

During the march on Washington, D.C., on August 28, 1963, in front of the Lincoln Memorial, the Reverend Dr. Martin Luther King, Jr., delivered his "I Have a Dream" speech. It is one of the great orations of the century, one of the world's most eloquent appeals for justice. The last lines are: "When we let freedom ring, when we let it ring from every village and every hamlet, from every state and every city, we will be able to speed up that day when all of God's children, black men, white men, Jews and gentiles, Protestants and Catholics, will be able to join hands and sing the words of the old Negro spiritual, 'Free at last! Free at last! Thank God Almighty, free at last!'"

THE LAST TIME WHISKEY OUTSOLD VODKA

The last time whiskey sales were higher than vodka sales in the United States was in 1972.

THE LAST OF THE STATE OF FRANKLIN

The state of Franklin, or Frankland, was formed on January 16, 1784, out of four North Carolina counties. John Sevier became governor. The state of North Carolina set up a separate government for the territory and much confusion followed until the area was ceded to the United States government in 1790. In 1796, it became the state of Tennessee.

The Last of the California Perfume Company

A New York City perfume company marketed its products door to door and last used the name California Perfume Company just before it celebrated its fiftieth anniversary and changed its name to Avon.

Number 4,208

The last buffalo killed by William Cody, Buffalo Bill.

The Last State of Ratify Prohibition

On January 16, 1919, Nebraska became the last state to ratify the Eighteenth Amendment, thus making it part of the United States Constitution.

The Last Time Virginia Was the Most Populous State

The last time the state of Virginia ranked as the most populous state in the United States of America was in the year 1800.

Last Time New York Was More Populous than California

The last time New York had more people than California was in 1940.

The Last Time Pennsylvania Was West New Jersey

June 30, 1676, was the last time Pennsylvania was called West New Jersey. However, New Jersey continued to have an "East" Jersey and a "West" Jersey until just before the Revolution. The dividing ran roughly from Perth Amboy to Trenton.

THE LAST OF THE *MAYFLOWER*

The *Mayflower* made her way back to England about 1621. On May 26, 1624, the court of admiralty, London, decreed the *Mayflower* of London to be scrapped. The owners, Robert Child, John Moore, and Christopher Jones's widow, sold the various parts of the ship—hull, mast, anchors, sails, muskets, pikes, shovels, etc.—for a total of £128, 8 shillings, and 4 pence.

THE LAST STATE OF THE THIRTEEN ORIGINAL STATES TO BE FOUNDED

Georgia was the last of the thirteen original states to be founded in America. In 1733 King George II of England granted a charter to James Oglethorpe, a British general, a member of Parliament, and a philanthropist, in order to provide a new home for the poor of England. Savannah became the first European settlement in what is now Georgia.

THE LAST OF THE ANTI-MASONIC PARTY

The first third party in United States history, the Anti-Masonic Party, was formed in 1827 to counter the alleged subversion of public institutions by the Freemasons. Hostility toward the Masons erupted following the 1826 disappearance and suspected murder in upstate New York of William Morgan, the author of a purported exposé of the Masons. The Anti-Masonic party rapidly gained followers, and in 1831 it held a national nominating convention in Baltimore—the first time that practice was followed. However, its presidential candidate, William Wirt, carried only one state (Vermont) in 1832, while Andrew Jackson, a Mason, won overwhelmingly. The last of the party came when they merged with the Whigs in 1839.

THE LAST TIME VERMONT WAS A COUNTRY
In 1777 Vermont wrote its own constitution and became an independent country. Its laws said that men could not own slaves and that you did not have to own property to vote. On March 4, 1781, it became the fourteenth state to be admitted to the union.

THE LAST SENTENCE OF THE DECLARATION OF INDEPENDENCE
"And for the support of the Declaration, with firm reliance on the protection of Divine Providence, we mutually pledge to each other our lives, our fortunes and our sacred honor."

THE LAST SENTENCE OF THE U.S. CONSTITUTION
"The ratification of the Conventions of nine States shall be sufficient for the Establishment of this Constitution between the States so ratifying the Same."

THE LAST LINE OF THE EMANCIPATION PROCLAMATION
Spoken by President Abraham Lincoln: "And upon this act, sincerely believed to be an act of justice, warranted by the Constitution, upon military necessity, I invoke the considerate judgment of mankind and the gracious favor of Almighty God."

THE LAST LINE OF THE FIRST STANZA OF "THE STAR-SPANGLED BANNER"
"Oh, say, does that star-spangled banner yet wave/O'er the land of the free and the home of the brave?"

The Lasts of
Ancient History

THE LAST BYZANTINE EMPEROR

Constantine XI ruled the Byzantine Empire from 1448 to 1453 A.D. He died fighting the Turks in the battle for Constantinople. The loss also marked the last of the 1,100-year old Byzantine Empire.

SOCRATES' LAST DAY

Socrates left no writings of his own. The Socratic method became known through the works of his pupil Plato. Socrates considered it his mission in life to question established assumptions through a process of proposition, argument, hypothesis, and deduction. In 399 B.C., Socrates was brought to trial for heresy and sentenced to die by poisoning. He was imprisoned for a month before his execution, and used the time to discourse as usual with his friends. The so-called prison, his last residence, was in the face of a cliff at the foot of Mouseion Hill. On Socrates' last day, described in Plato's dialogue *Phaedo*, he drank hemlock and died.

THE LAST TIME HIPPOS WADDLED IN THE THAMES RIVER, ENGLAND

Between the last two glacial epochs, the climate melted enough polar ice to raise sea levels some 30 feet. As noted by a member of the British Antarctic Survey team, Dr. David Peelt, it was so warm in England that hippopotamuses wallowed in the Thames and lions roamed its banks.

THE LAST ANCIENT OLYMPIC GAMES

The ancient Greek games were held in the summer at Olympia once every four years starting in 776 B.C. They were held in honor of Zeus. The last games were held in 397 B.C. and were banned by Emperor Theodosius of Rome in 393 B.C.

THE LAST LEGAL BACCHANALIA

It was in the second century B.C. The Roman Senate banned this festival honoring Bacchus, the Roman god of wine. It was originally a religious rite celebrated only by women, but eventually it included men and became an excuse for drunken orgies.

THE LAST LEGAL GLADIATORIAL FIGHT

The Roman emperor Constantine the Great abolished gladiatorial contests in 325 A.D., but they continued. Honorius tried to abolish them again in the fifth century, and once more failed. No date is known for the last such contest.

THE LAST OF THE TWELVE LABORS OF HERCULES

The last of the twelve labors of Hercules was to bring back the golden apples of the Hesperides, the daughters of Atlas who lived in a wonderful garden on the western edge of the world. With the help of Ladon the dragon, they guarded a tree that bore golden apples. Hercules slew the dragon and got the golden apples. Another source has Eurystheus giving Hercules twelve seemingly impossible tasks to complete, the last of which was to bring Cerberus up from Hades.

THE LAST OF THE GOTHS

The Goths were a Germanic people who lived in central Europe. An uncivilized, fierce, and barbaric race, they were bold fighters and stern rulers. They fought the Romans in 410 A.D. and took over the Roman capital for a short period. They often settled down in the places they invaded, and in 553 A.D., the last of the Goths merged with tribes in Northern Europe and disappeared as a nation.

THE LAST WOMAN PHARAOH

The eighteenth-dynasty Egyptian queen Hatshepsut became regent for her son after the death of her husband, Thutmose II (c. 1504 B.C.). In 1503 B.C. she became the last (and only) woman pharaoh. She was very progressive and sponsored commercial and building programs, including the temple at Deir el-Bahri.

THE LAST KING OF THE FIRST WORLD EMPIRE

In 549 B.C. Persia was ruled by the Achaemenids. Named after
an eponymous ancestor, Achaemenes, they were Persian kings
who ruled over the first empire of the world, from the Aegean
Sea to the Indus River. Under the Achaemenids' rule, universal
law (king's law) and a postal and coinage system were established. Cyrus the Great was the first Achaemenid ruler of Persia, but Darius I was the real builder of the Persian empire.
Darius III became the last king when he was defeated by
Alexander the Great in 330 B.C.

Last Times

802,701 A.D.

The last stop by the Time Traveller in H. G. Wells's *The Time Machine* was the year 802,701 A.D.

OUR SUN WAS TWENTY-ONE ON ITS LAST BIRTHDAY

The sun is between twenty and twenty-one cosmic years old. A cosmic year is the length of time it takes the sun to complete one revolution around the center of the Milky Way galaxy, about 225 million years.

THE LAST YEAR THE CALENDAR WILL HAVE 365 DAYS

The last year the calendar with have 365 days and 366 for leap year will be in the year 5315 A.D. Over the next 3,323 years the earth's orbit will add 26 seconds per year, so that by the year 5316 A.D. another day will be added to the year—366 days and 367 for leap year. Notice: whoever is in charge of calendars in the fifty-fourth century, please add a long weekend in August.

LAST CHRISTMAS OF THE TWENTIETH CENTURY
The last Christmas in the twentieth century will fall on Monday, December 25, 2000. Most companies have not yet decided whether employees will have the following Tuesday off.

THE LAST DAY OF THE JULIAN CALENDAR
October 4, 1582. The next day was October 15, 1582, in the new Gregorian calendar. Pope Gregory XIII reformed the calendar, replacing the inaccurate Julian calendar, which lost time.

THE LAST TIME THERE WAS A MONTH WITHOUT A FULL MOON
The last time there was a month without a full moon was in February of 1866. The next time there will be a month without a full moon will be in the year 2,501,991 A.D.

Holy Moly Lasts

THE LAST JUDGMENT

The last judgment of mankind before God at the end of the world is said to be scheduled for various dates, according to different cult spokespersons. William Miller (1782–1849) predicted the end of the world for 1843, then for 1844. When it did not occur, the Seventh Day Adventists adopted a statement declaring their belief in the visible return of Christ at an indefinite time.

THE LAST SUPPER

Passover meal taken by Jesus and his disciples on the eve of the passion (Matthew 26:17–30; Mark 14:12–26; Luke 22:7–39; John 13–17; I Corinthians 1:23–29).

THE LAST HORSEMAN

The last horseman of the Apocalypse is Death, according to Revelations 6:2–8. The others were War, Famine, and Pestilence.

THE FIRST SHALL BE LAST

"Many that are first shall be last; and the last shall be first."
—Matthew 19:30.

THE LAST TIME MARTIN LUTHER WAS A CATHOLIC

The last day Martin Luther, an Augustinian friar, was a Roman Catholic was January 6, 1521. The next day he was formally excommunicated, and summoned to appear before the Diet of Worms. His friends placed him for safekeeping in Wartburg at the Castle of Elector Frederick III of Saxony. There Luther translated the New Testament into German and began the translation of the entire Bible, which took ten years.

THE LAST OF THE FOUR BASIC GOALS OF HINDUISM

Moksha, spiritual liberation.

THE LAST WORDS OF THE PROPHET JOSEPH SMITH

The last words uttered by the founder of the Church of Jesus Christ of the Latter Day Saints, as he leaped from the second-story window of the jail in Carthage, Illinois, amidst a hail of gunfire from the murderous mob below, were "Oh, Lord my God."

THE LAST QUAKER EXECUTED IN BOSTON

The last Quaker to be executed in Boston, Massachusetts, was William Laddra on March 24, 1661. He suffered the death penalty when he illegally returned from banishment.

THE LAST TIME THE EPISCOPAL CHURCH HAD ONLY MALE PRIESTS

The last time the Episcopal Church had only male priests was in 1978. In 1979 four Episcopal bishops defied church law and ordained eleven women as priests.

BUDDHA'S LAST NAME

Buddha was the founder of Buddhism in India in the sixth to fifth century B.C. His given name was Siddhartha and his last name was Gautama or Gotama.

THE LAST OF THE TRIBES OF ISRAEL

The last two Hebrew tribes, the tribes of Benjamin and Judah, are the founders of the kingdom of Judah. The kingdom of Israel was formed in 930 B.C. by ten of the twelve original Hebrew tribes. The kingdom was conquered by the Assyrians in 721 B.C. Those tribes were exiled and dispersed to assimilate into other nations.

THE LAST OF THE HOLY ROMAN EMPIRE

The Holy Roman Empire, which was founded by Charlemagne in 800 A.D., saw its last days when it was abolished in 1806 under pressure from Napoleon.

THE LAST CHILDREN'S CRUSADE

There were two children's crusades, both in 1212 A.D. The last was led by a boy preacher named Nicholas who led thousands of German children as far as Italy; they were turned back.

THE LAST AMEN

The last of the 773,692 words in the King James Bible is "The grace of our lord Jesus Christ be with you all. Amen." —Revelation 22:21.

THE LAST CRUSADE

The last crusade was in 1396. A crusaders' army under the leadership of the Hungarian King Sigismund (later emperor) and the Burgundian Prince John Without Fear battled the Turks near Nikopolis and were defeated. Louis IX, however, called his crusade to Tunis in 1270 A.D. the seventh and last crusade, and historians still inaccurately call it so.

CHRIST'S LAST WORDS ON THE CROSS

Jesus spoke seven times on the cross, according to the Gospels of the New Testament. His last saying, from Luke 23:46, was "Father, into thy hands I commend my spirit."

THE LAST GREEK POPE OF ROME

The last Greek to be pope of the Roman Catholic Chuch was Alexander V, who reigned from 1409 until he died the following year.

THE LAST SUNDAY IN JULY

On the last Sunday in July, Irish Catholics, by tradition, do penance by climbing Croagh Patrick, a 2,510-foot mountain where Saint Patrick is supposed to have begun his missionary work.

THE LAST STATION OF THE CROSS
There are fourteen shrines or Stations of the Cross marking the episodes that occurred during the Passion of Christ. The last station is "the burial of His body."

TWO LAST COMMANDMENTS
Of the ten commandments given to Moses by God on Mount Sinai, there are two versions of the last commandment, one followed by Roman Catholics and Lutherans: "Thou shalt not covet thy neighbor's property," the other followed by most Protestants and the Eastern Orthodox religions: "Thou shalt not covet thy neighbor's wife and his property."

SAINT THOMAS AQUINAS'S LAST STOP
Saint Thomas Aquinas, the great medieval scholar, was born in Roccasecca, Italy, in the family castle of the counts of Aquino, in 1225. His last stop en route to the Council of Lyon was a tenth-century Cistercian abbey; he died there in 1274 before he could complete his trip.

THE LAST OF SODOM AND GOMORRAH
In Genesis 19, God destroyed the two "cities of the plain" with a rain of "fire and brimstone" as punishment for their evil ways. Archaeologists place Sodom and Gomorrah at the southern end of the Dead Sea and guess that an earthquake demolished them around 1900 B.C.

The Lasts of Battles and Wars

NAPOLEON'S LAST BATTLE

The last battle of Napoleon Bonaparte was fought at Waterloo on June 18, 1815, where he was defeated. It was the battle that finally ended the war and his career.

THE LAST OF NAPOLEON'S ELEMENTS OF WAR

Napoleon Bonaparte's fifth and last element of war was "Mud."

THE LAST OF THE UNITED STATES GROUND TROOPS LEAVE VIETNAM

On March 29, 1973, the last of the United States ground troops left Vietnam.

THE LAST OF THE SPANISH CIVIL WAR

After three years of internal strife Generalissimo Francisco Franco brought the Spanish Civil War to a triumphant end on March 28, 1939, when his Nationalists defeated the Loyalist Republicans. The United States soon recognized the new Spanish government.

THE LAST OF THE FIRST PRISONER-OF-WAR CAMP

In England, Norman Cross Depot near Stilton in Huntington-shire was the first prisoner-of-war camp, housing prisoners captured in the Napoleonic wars. It closed in 1802 when peace was declared but reopened when hostilities were renewed in 1803. The forty-acre camp was demolished in 1816.

THE LAST GORILLA HANGED AS A SPY

In 1705, on the beach of West Hartlepool, England, some people from the village saw a hairy-looking stranger get out of a rowboat. They couldn't understand its jabbering and had never seen an ape before. It was captured, court-martialed, and hanged as a French spy. Britain was at war with France at the time, and the ape was the mascot of a wrecked warship.

THE LAST TIME CATS WERE USED AS AMMUNITION

In the 6th century B.C., King Cambyses II of Persia advanced against the city of Memphis and was chagrined to find the city walls too high and thick for a conventional assault. The Persian warriors were then instructed to go on a massive hunt for cats. The captured felines were hurled over city walls and landed on the heads of outraged Egyptians. Because Egyptians worshiped these creatures, they were unwilling to see divine animals so cruelly treated, and they surrendered, even though they had superior force. In 525 B.C., Cambyses II put a row of cats on the front lines of his army. Egyptian archers refused to shoot their arrows for fear of killing the venerated felines.

HANNIBAL'S LAST NAME

Barca. Hannibal, the Carthaginian general, was born in Sicily in 247 B.C. His father, the defender of Sicily in the first Punic War, was Hamilcar Barca.

THE LAST SURVIVORS OF THE ALAMO

Under the dual leadership of W. B. Travis and Jim Bowie, varying estimates of 182, 188, or 253 Texans held old Fort Alamo in San Antonio for thirteen days against Mexican president-general Santa Anna. The garrison finally surrendered on March 6, 1836, when all but seven had been killed. These last survivors, including Davy Crockett, were shot or hacked to death with sabers on the orders of Santa Anna. On April 21, at San Jacinto, General Sam Houston crushed Santa Anna and drove his troops out of Texas and back to Mexico. "Remember the Alamo" became the war cry for Texas independence.

PT-109'S LAST MISSION

In the dark, early morning hours of August 2, 1943, fifteen American patrol-torpedo boats were assigned the task of trying to block the almost nightly fleet of Japanese destroyers bringing reinforcements to the Central Solomon Islands. The action took place at Blackett Strait, south of the island of Kolomban-gara. The American PT boats fired torpedoes lavishly without scoring a hit. But Japanese naval Commander Hanami of the destroyer *Amagiri* succeeded in running down and knifing in two boat PT-109, commanded by Lieutenant John F. Kennedy, USNR. Eleven members of the boat's crew of thirteen survived, including Kennedy, who seventeen years later was elected president of the United States.

THE LAST SURVIVOR OF THE CREW OF PT-109
Gerald Zinser of Naples, Florida, is the last surviving member of the PT-109 crew.

THE LAST WAR IN SWEDEN'S HISTORY
Neutrality is the keystone of modern Sweden's relations with the world. The country has kept out of wars since 1814, when Norway resisted union with Sweden.

THE LAST DAY OF AMERICAN HOSTAGES IN IRAN
January 20, 1981. After being held hostage for 444 days in Teheran, Iran, the fifty-two Americans were released on the day Ronald Reagan was inaugurated.

CUSTER'S LASTS
General George Armstrong Custer had the dubious honor of finishing last in his graduating class at West Point. In 1861, the future general ranked thirty-fifth out of a graduating class of thirty-five students. The last fort where Custer was sta-tioned was Fort Abraham Lincoln in Dakota Territory. His last

command was the 7th U.S. Cavalry Regiment, and his Last Stand, on June 25, 1876, was at the Battle of the Little Bighorn, where Custer died with 264 of his men.

LAST SURVIVOR OF THE BATTLE OF THE LITTLE BIGHORN

The last and only United States survivor of the Battle of the Little Bighorn was Comanche, a horse. His rider, Captain Myles W. Keogh, was killed along with Custer and 263 of the other soldiers. The horse suffered seven wounds, including three serious ones in the neck, lung, and groin. He survived to become a legend. He was sent to Fort Lincoln, Dakota Territory, and by special order no one was allowed to ride him. He was paraded at ceremonies and was free to wander at each post he attended. At thirty years old, Comanche died of colic at Fort Riley, Kansas, on November 9, 1893.

THE LAST OF THE PELOPONNESIAN WARS

The last day of the Peloponnesian wars was April 25, 404 B.C. When Athens ran out of food supplies, it surrendered to Sparta, thus ending the wars that started in 432 B.C.

THE LAST CAVALRY

The horse cavalry in the United States dates back to the American Revolution. Only four horse cavalry regiments saw service in France in World War I. Armored tanks replaced horses after the war, offering greater mobility and firepower. The 26th Cavalry Regiment of the Philippine Scouts was the last mounted unit to see action. The 26th shot at the invading Japanese forces in the Philippines in December 1941 and covered the

American retreat to Bataan. On January 15, 1942, they made their last stand against the Japanese, then retreated to Bataan, where the men were forced to slaughter their horses for food.

THE LAST TIME THE UNITED STATES OF AMERICA DID NOT HAVE AN ARMY

Immediately after the end of the American Revolutionary War, Congress abolished the United States Army, the Navy, and the Marine Corps because the states feared a standing national army. Congress became the only national governmental organization.

THE LAST UNITED STATES BATTLES WHERE THE FLAG WASN'T FLOWN

Until 1834, only regimental colors were taken into war. In 1834, Congress awarded the privilege of flying the United States flags in battle to American artillery units only. Then in late 1876 the U.S. Marines were allowed to carry the flag, and the cavalry followed in 1887.

LITTLE AMERICA LAST USED AS A UNITED STATES BASE

Little America in Antarctica was last used as a United States military base in 1958. It was abandoned that year in favor of a better location.

THE LAST BATTLE OF THE SPANISH-AMERICAN WAR

The last battle began on July 1, 1898, at El Caney and San Juan Hill. The Rough Riders, 1st Regiment of U.S. Cavalry Volunteers, led by Leonard Wood and Theodore Roosevelt, won their heroic reputation in this conflict.

LAST BATTLE OF THE WAR OF 1812

The last battle of this war took place after the signing of the Treaty of Ghent (December 24, 1814) had officially ended the war. On January 8, 1815, Andrew Jackson decisively defeated the British at New Orleans.

THE LAST YEAR OF THE HUNDRED YEARS' WAR

The war started in Crécy in northern France in 1346. In the war's last year, 1453, the French, inspired by Joan of Arc, fought hard and finally beat back the British, who lost all the land they had won on the continent.

The Lasts of the American Revolution

THE LAST BATTLE OF THE REVOLUTIONARY WAR

In the last battle of the Revolutionary War, Cornwallis was defeated at Yorktown in October 1781.

THE LAST VICTIM OF THE BOSTON MASSACRE

The Boston Massacre grew out of the colonials' resentment of the British troops sent to Boston to enforce the Townshend Acts and to maintain law and order. (The Townshend Acts were passed by the British Parliament after the repeal of the Stamp Act, to collect revenues from the colonists in America on imports of lead, glass, paints, tea, and paper.) Gangs of irresponsible citizens constantly harassed the troops, who were not allowed to fire on them without the order of a civil authority. Finally, on March 5, 1770, battered by a rioting crowd near what is now the Old State House, a unit of soldiers fired. Five men died as a result, three the first day: Crispus Attucks,

Sam Gray, and James Caldwell; Samuel Maverick died the next day, and nine days later, Patrick Carr became the last to die. In addition, eleven men were injured.

THE LAST SURVIVOR OF THE BOSTON TEA PARTY

David Kennison, born in 1736, lived to be 115 years old. The British Parliament, which had suffered many setbacks in its attempts to control its colonies in the New World, had retained the tea tax as a symbol of its right to tax the colonies. In Boston three ships arrived in the harbor, but the governor would not let them unload without paying the tea tax. On the night of December 6, 1773, a group of incensed colonists disguised as Indians, led by Paul Revere, Samuel Adams, and others, including the thirty-seven-year-old Kennison, boarded the ships and threw the tea into Boston Harbor. Kennison went on to serve in the Revolutionary War, and at the age of seventy-five served in the War of 1812. He lived a very active life and spent his last days in Illinois, where he died peacefully in 1851.

LAST SIGNER OF THE DECLARATION OF INDEPENDENCE

Thomas McKean, delegate from Delaware, did not sign until 1781 by special permission of Congress, having served in the army in the interim. McKean was a Delaware jurist and president of the Continental Congress in 1781, when the Articles of Confederation were adopted upon Maryland's ratification. He is sometimes called the first president of the United States of America.

THE LAST SURVIVING SIGNER OF THE
DECLARATION OF INDEPENDENCE

Charles Carroll of Carrollton signed the Declaration of Independence on August 2, 1776. Of the fifty-nine signers of the Declaration of Independence, Carroll was the last to die. He passed away in 1832, at the age of ninety-five.

THE LAST DAYS OF BENEDICT ARNOLD

Benedict Arnold, American revolutionary general and traitor, spent his last days in England, where he was generally scorned and unrewarded. He died in 1801.

NATHAN HALE'S LAST WORDS

When he was about to be hanged by the British in 1776, he is said to have uttered "I only regret that I have but one life to lose for my country." However, British officer Captain Frederick Mackenzie recorded in his diary that what Hale actually said was "It is the duty of every good officer to obey any orders given him by his commander in chief."

THE LAST SURVIVING VETERAN OF THE REVOLUTIONARY WAR

The last surviving soldier of the Revolutionary War was John Gray, who had worked for George Washington at Mount Vernon and was present when Cornwallis surrendered at Yorktown. He died in Hiramsburg, Ohio, on March 29, 1868, at the age of 104.

THE LAST STATE OF THE THIRTEEN ORIGINAL STATES TO
RATIFY THE CONSTITUTION

Rhode Island, May 29, 1790.

Lasts in World History

COLUMBUS'S LAST RESTING PLACE

Both Spain and Santo Domingo claim to be the home of the remains of the great discoverer.

LAST REWARDS

Some of history's most renowned explorers' last rewards left a lot to be desired:

• Vasco Nunez de Balboa, Spanish explorer, discoverer of the Pacific Ocean. In 1519 he was accused of treason and beheaded in Spain.

• Vitus J. Bering, Danish explorer in Russian employ. Shipwrecked on the shore of Bering Island and died there December 8, 1741, of scurvy.

• Captain James Cook, English explorer and navigator, was ambushed and slain by natives in the Sandwich (Hawaiian) Islands in 1779.

• Hernando Cortés, Spanish conquistador and conqueror of Mexico. In 1547 he died in Spain, neglected by the court and hurt by King Charles V's refusal to name him Governor of Mexico.

• Sir Francis Drake, English navigator and admiral, first Englishman to circumnavigate the world. In 1596 during his last expedition, a venture against the Spanish in the West Indies, which was a complete failure, Drake died of dysentery off the coast of Portobello and was buried at sea.

• Henry Hudson, English navigator and explorer. His discoveries gave England claim to the Hudson Bay region. In the summer of 1611 his starved and diseased crew mutinied and set Hudson, his son, and seven of his men adrift in Hudson Bay, without food or water; they were never seen again.

• Meriwether Lewis, American explorer, one of the leaders of the Lewis and Clark expedition, governor of Louisiana Territory. In 1809, while traveling to Washington, D.C., he died suddenly, either by suicide or murder, in a lonely inn on the Natchez Trace, a road from Natchez, Mississippi, to Nashville, Tennessee.

• Francisco Pizarro, Spanish conquistador and conqueror of Peru. Pizarro's greed, ambition, and the cheating and killing of his partner Almagro got the best of him. In 1541 a band of assassins, sympathtic to Almagro, surprised him at dinner and killed him.

• Robert Cavelier, Sieur de La Salle. This French explorer of North America was murdered in 1687 by his own men, who mutinied after many futile attempts to find the mouth of the Mississippi River overland.

•Pedro de Valdivia, Spanish explorer, conqueror of Chile. Forty of Valdivia's men were captured by Araucanian Indians and massacred. Lautaro, the leader of the Indians, forced Valdivia to swallow molten gold, killing him.

THE LAST OF THE AZTEC EMPIRE

The Aztec Empire fell on August 13, 1521, when Hernando Cortés conquered the Aztec capital of Tenochtitlan after a three-month siege.

THE LAST MAGNA CARTA

There were actually three issues of the Magna Carta after the first one was forced on King John at Runnymede by the barons and the church on June 9, 1215. The last one, issued in 1225, was the one incorporated into British law.

RALEIGH'S LAST TRIP TO THE TOWER OF LONDON

Sir Walter Raleigh, explorer and pirate for Queen Elizabeth I of England, returned from North America with tobacco and started the world on the road to lung cancer. For several years he attended the royal court but earned the queen's displeasure after he quarreled with her favorite, the earl of Essex. After Elizabeth's death, James I sent Sir Walter to the Tower of London for the third and last time. (The first two times were for a forbidden marriage and an intrigue with Spain.) After a brief trial he was executed on October 29, 1618.

LAST NAME OF ENGLISH LAND AGENT WHOSE EMPLOYEES REFUSED TO WORK FOR HIM

Boycott. Charles Boycott, an English estate manager in the 1880s, used rent-collection tactics so outrageous that his Irish tenants refused to harvest his crops.

THE LAST OF THE EASTER ISLANDERS

Easter Island is one of the most remote places in the world. Easter Islanders evolved a form of writing uniquely their own, developed a system of solar observations, and brought rock and cave painting to a high art. In a 900-year period they also produced over 1,000 stone heads, called *moai*, for which the island is famous. The *moai* are huge, ranging from 12 feet high to 32 feet long and weighing 80 tons. One unfinished head abandoned at the quarry site is 60 feet long and weighs about 270 tons.

Between 1859 and 1862 Peruvian slavers captured 2,000 of the inhabitants of Easter Island, including the king and his son, and took them to Peru in South America. The Easter Islanders never recovered from this shock to their culture. The few who survived their servitude and returned to Easter Island brought back diseases for which the remaining natives had no resistance. By 1877, native Easter Islanders numbered no more than 150. When these last holders of the ancient traditions died, the knowledge of how the giant *moai* were made and erected died with them.

THE LAST DAY OF THE INCA EMPIRE

The last day of the magnificent Inca Empire was November 18, 1533. The next day it fell to Francisco Pizarro and his army.

THE LAST LEFT-OR-RIGHT-FOOT SHOES, OR, THE FIRST LEFT AND RIGHT SHOE LASTS

Prior to 1818 shoes were made so that they would fit the left or right foot. In 1818 the left shoe "last" (or form) and the right shoe "last" were invented so that each shoe had a custom fit.

GORBACHEV'S LAST DAY AS PRIME MINISTER OF THE U.S.S.R.

Michael Gorbachev's last day as Prime Minister of the Soviet Union was December 24, 1991. He was succeeded by Boris Yeltsin.

THE LAST OF THE U.S.S.R.

The Union of Soviet Socialist Republics broke up into fifteen independent countries in 1992.

Potpourri Lasts

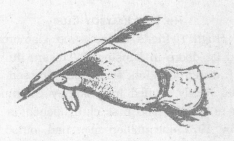

THE LAST WORDS OF DR. GREEN
The last words of Dr. Joseph Green, after taking his own pulse: "Stopped."

THE LAST BONE IN THE SPINAL COLUMN
The last bone at the bottom of the spinal column is called the coccyx.

THE PROCRASTINATORS NEWSLETTER
The Procrastinators Club of America sends news to its members under the masthead "Last Month's Newsletter."

THE LAST NUMBER ADDED TO THE MATHEMATICS SYSTEM
Zero was the last number added to mathematics. The lack of zero was one of the drawbacks of Greek mathematics. The

Arabs passed it to on to European mathematicians in the later part of the Middle Ages. The Arabs obtained the symbol from the Hindus. The Mayas of Central America and the Babylonians developed zero independently.

THE LAST PLAYBOY CLUB

The last of Hugh Hefner's famous and glamorous Playboy Clubs closed its doors in Lansing, Michigan, July 31, 1988. The clubs featured cocktail waitresses dressed as Playboy Bunnies, just barely stuffed into skimpy costumes that included ears and tails. The first club opened in Chicago in 1960, and by 1972 one million men had joined twenty-two clubs around the world.

THE FINAL RESTING PLACE OF THE CARDIFF GIANT

The Cardiff Giant, supposedly the remains of a primitive man, but in fact a hoax, changed ownership many times over the years. Finally in 1948, eighty years after it was carved, it arrived at its last resting place: the Farmers Museum in Cooperstown, New York.

THE LAST SYLLABLE OF THE CAMPFIRE GIRLS' WATCHWORD

Love. The Campfire Girls' watchword, "Wohelo," is made up of the first two letters each of Work, Health, and Love.

THE LAST OF THE GLAGOLITIC ALPHABET

The Glagolitic alphabet disappeared in the seventeenth century, except for liturgical use in parts of the former Yugoslavia. Saints Cyril and Methodius were Greek missionaries and inventors of the Cyrillic and Glagolitic alphabets for the Slavs. Only the Cyrillic alphabet is still in common use.

THE LAST OF THE NINETEENTH-CENTURY COMIC STRIPS
The Katzenjammer Kids is the oldest surviving comic strip. Created in 1897, it is still running in newspapers all over the world.

SANTA'S LAST REINDEER
In Clement Clark Moore's poem, "A Visit from St. Nicholas," written in 1823, the last of the eight tiny reindeer is Blitzen.

THE LAST PLACE IN MONOPOLY
The last place in the board game of Monopoly is Boardwalk. After that, you pass Go and collect $200.

PANDORA'S BOX
The last thing to escape Pandora's box was Hope.

THE LAST MUSKETEER
Gascon nobleman D'Artagnan was the last to join Athos, Porthos, and Aramis in the many adventures of Alexandre Dumas's Three Musketeers.

THE LAST OF THE DANDIES
A title given to French Count Alfred Guillaume Gabriel D'Orsay (1801–1852), the son of a Bonapartist general who went to England in 1821, becoming the center of a fashionable artistic

and literary circle in London. D'Orsay was long the authority on matters of taste in English society, but was forced to flee to Paris in 1849 to escape his creditors.

THE LAST OF THE ENGLISH

Hereward the Wake, who led the failed uprising of the English at Ely against William the Conqueror, was called the last of the English.

THE LAST MAN

Charles I was so-called by the parliamentarians, who predicted that he would be the last king of Great Britain. His son Charles II was called the Son of the Last Man.

ALPHABETS' LAST LETTERS

Greek: Omega
Cyrillic: Ya (Я)
Arabic: Ya (y)
Sanskrit: ha
Phoenician: Tav

THE LAST LETTERS ADDED TO THE ENGLISH ALPHABET

J and V.

LAST NAMES IN THE PHONE BOOK

Albany, New York . . . Zywotow, Marvin
Atlanta, Georgia . . . Zzmmthisj, Zibre
Austin, Texas . . . Zzyou, Bob

Boston, Masschusetts . . . Zzzyli, Z.

Bronx, New York . . . Zymeck, Rudolph

Cincinnati, Ohio . . . Zyromski, Kristiana

Cleveland, Ohio . . . Zyzniewski, Ray

Daytona Beach (Area), Florida . . . Zymalski, H. V.

Daytona Beach (and Vicinity), Florida . . . Zyznomyrsky, J.

District of Columbia . . . Zzylch, R.

Houston, Texas . . . Zwieg, Larry & Susan

Jacksonville, Florida . . . Zwink, Randall

Kansas City, Kansas . . . Zzzent, Zebo

Lansing, Michigan . . . Zyskowski, John

Manhattan, New York . . . Zzzzzip, Zelmo

Mobile, Alabama . . . Zisman, Walt

Oklahoma City, Oklahoma . . . Zyzak, Richard H.

Pittsburgh, Pennsylvania . . . Zyzzak, Zackery

Providence, Rhode Island . . . Zywien, David L.

Queens, New York . . . Zzzzzzzzzzzzzzzzzzzzzzz (That's 23 Z's)

Sacramento, California . . . Zysk, Sophie F.

Seattle, Washington . . . Zysom, K.

Stockton, California . . . Zylla, T.

Miami, Florida . . . Zzzzyzman, Josef

Fort Lauderdale, Florida . . . Zzymo, Bert

San Antonio, Texas . . . Zzackey, Dennis & Patty

Toronto, Canada . . . Zzcura, C. J. . . . Zzootz Hair Design

FOR THE BEST IN PAPERBACKS, LOOK FOR THE

In every corner of the world, on every subject under the sun, Penguin represents quality and variety—the very best in publishing today.

For complete information about books available from Penguin—including Puffins, Penguin Classics, and Arkana—and how to order them, write to us at the appropriate address below. Please note that for copyright reasons the selection of books varies from country to country.

In the United Kingdom: Please write to *Dept. JC, Penguin Books Ltd, FREEPOST, West Drayton, Middlesex UB7 0BR.*

If you have any difficulty in obtaining a title, please send your order with the correct money, plus ten percent for postage and packaging, to *P.O. Box No. 11, West Drayton, Middlesex UB7 0BR*

In the United States: Please write to *Consumer Sales, Penguin USA, P.O. Box 999, Dept. 17109, Bergenfield, New Jersey 07621-0120.* VISA and MasterCard holders call 1-800-253-6476 to order all Penguin titles

In Canada: Please write to *Penguin Books Canada Ltd, 10 Alcorn Avenue, Suite 300, Toronto, Ontario M4V 3B2*

In Australia: Please write to *Penguin Books Australia Ltd, P.O. Box 257, Ringwood, Victoria 3134*

In New Zealand: Please write to *Penguin Books (NZ) Ltd, Private Bag 102902, North Shore Mail Centre, Auckland 10*

In India: Please write to *Penguin Books India Pvt Ltd, 706 Eros Apartments, 56 Nehru Place, New Delhi 110 019*

In the Netherlands: Please write to *Penguin Books Netherlands bv, Postbus 3507, NL-1001 AH Amsterdam*

In Germany: Please write to *Penguin Books Deutschland GmbH, Metzlerstrasse 26, 60594 Frankfurt am Main*

In Spain: Please write to *Penguin Books S.A., Bravo Murillo 19, 1° B, 28015 Madrid*

In Italy: Please write to *Penguin Italia s.r.l., Via Felice Casati 20, I-20124 Milano*

In France: Please write to *Penguin France S.A., 17 rue Lejeune, F-31000 Toulouse*

In Japan: Please write to *Penguin Books Japan, Ishikiribashi Building, 2-5-4, Suido, Bunkyo-ku, Tokyo 112*

In Greece: Please write to *Penguin Hellas Ltd, Dimocritou 3, GR-106 71 Athens*

In South Africa: Please write to *Longman Penguin Southern Africa (Pty) Ltd, Private Bag X08, Bertsham 2013*